Here's to the *Crazy* Entrepreneurs

Is Entrepreneurism a Mental Disorder?

Foreword by Robert S. Rippy

Stephen C. Harper, Ph.D.

Library of Congress Cataloging-in-Publishing Data:

Harper, Stephen C.

Here's to the crazy entrepreneurs: Is entrepreneurism a mental disorder? / Stephen C. Harper: Foreword by Robert S. Rippy.

Includes bibliographic references

ISBN-13: 978-1491259238
ISBN-10: 149125923X

Entrepreneurship. 2. Leadership. 3. Management. 4. Innovation. 1. Title.

Library of Congress Control Number: 2013914347

This book is also available on the World Wide Web as an e-Book.

Stephen C. Harper Publisher

Manufactured in the United States of America

CreateSpace, North Charleston, SC.

This book is dedicated to the entrepreneurs who ignore the naysayers who say, "Are you crazy?" By sensing and seizing opportunities, entrepreneurs transform problems in the marketplace into businesses that "make a dent in the universe." They are the ones who enhance the quality of our lives and make the world a better place.

It is also dedicated to Bob Rippy who presented his "The Dark Side of Entrepreneurship" to my students over the years and the other entrepreneurs I have known who reminded me that entrepreneurism is a mental disorder that should not be cured!

Contents

Acknowledgments   7

Profile of the Author   9

FOREWORD by Robert S. Rippy – Serial Entrepreneur   11

PREFACE   13

INTRODUCTION   17

CHAPTER ONE: Entrepreneurs are not like normal people   21

CHAPTER TWO: The role of mental health in entrepreneurism   45

CHAPTER THREE: A closer look at mental disorders   67

CHAPTER FOUR: Serial entrepreneurs and multipreneurs: One startup is not enough   81

CHAPTER FIVE: Helping entrepreneurs cope with their situations   97

EPILOGUE: Thank goodness for entrepreneurs   117

References   121

Acknowledgments

I want to thank Dan and Betty Cameron for establishing the Progress Energy/Betty Cameron Distinguished Professorship of Entrepreneurship at The University of North Carolina Wilmington. The endowed professorship has given me the opportunity to write this book and to pursue numerous other activities to help entrepreneurs and to enhance the education for my students. I also want to thank Larry Clark - Dean of the Cameron School of Business at the University of North Carolina Wilmington. Dean Clark has been supportive of everything I have done. His unlimited energy and enthusiasm for entrepreneurship education over the years have been sources of inspiration for me as I enter my fifth decade as an educator.

I want to thank three other groups for making my professional journey so rewarding. First, I want to thank the students I have worked with at The University of North Carolina Wilmington, Duke University, and Arizona State University. Second, I want to thank the entrepreneurs who over the last two decades have elevated being an entrepreneur from being a social outcast to being a role model for how to sense and seize opportunities as well as how to foster innovation. They have changed how we live and work.

Third, I want to thank the entrepreneurs and executives I have known personally. They have provided me with insights into today's challenges of starting and growing businesses. They have taught me a lot about various industries, markets, and firms. They have helped me see the world from various perspectives. It would be nearly impossible for me to list all of the entrepreneurs I have known who have had a profound impact on my thinking about creativity, innovation, education, taking risks, and so forth. I would like to note a few in particular, however, at the risk of leaving many out. Bob Rippy has demonstrated how to mentor entrepreneurs. Chad Paul whose unbridled energy and insights are contagious. Tom Looney who has shown me what passion and perseverance are all about. Tobin Geatz who has shown me the value of candor. Dr. Roy Archambault who always puts a smile on my face and has shown me what unbridled curiosity and creativity look like. Brett Martin who has demonstrated an incredible commitment to helping students better understand the entrepreneurial journey. Dave Phillips showed me what an outlier really looks like. And last but not least, Buddy Beck who has demonstrated that real entrepreneurs never run out of ideas and there is no such thing as retirement!

Many of the entrepreneurs I have known have enhanced the quality of education where I have taught by being guest speakers, advisory board members, business plan jurors, internship sponsors, visiting entrepreneurs, and in numerous other areas. Their enthusiasm has inspired my students. Their advice has been very helpful to me and my students.

As always, I want to thank my family for bringing joy to my life.

About the Author

Stephen C. Harper, Ph.D., is the Progress Energy/Betty Cameron Distinguished Professor of Entrepreneurship at The University of North Carolina Wilmington. Steve is the author of the following books on entrepreneurship and leadership:

- *Taking Your Business to the Next Level and Beyond: The Entrepreneur's Guide to Developing an Exceptional Enterprise* (2012)
- *The Ever-Evolving Enterprise: Guidelines for Creating Your Company's Future* (2011)
- *Extraordinary Entrepreneurship : The Professional's Guide to Starting an Exceptional Enterprise* (2005)
- *The McGraw-Hill Guide to Starting Your Own Business: A Step-by-Step Blueprint for the First-Time Entrepreneur* (2005 & 1991)
- *The Forward-Focused Organization: Visionary Thinking and Breakthrough Leadership to Create Your Company's Future* (2001)
- *The McGraw-Hill Guide to Managing Growth in Your Emerging Business: Guidelines for Transforming Your Small Business Into an Exceptional Enterprise* (1995)
- *Management: Who Ever Said It Would Be Easy?* Editor and Co-Author (1983)
- He is also the author of dozens of articles that have appeared in national and international magazines.

He is the recipient of numerous awards including: The University of North Carolina Board of Governors' Award for Teaching Excellence, The University of North Carolina Wilmington's Distinguished Teaching Professorship Award, The Board of Trustees'

Teaching Excellence Award, and the Chancellor's Teaching Excellence Award.

He has also received The Award for Faculty Scholarship at UNCW as well as the Chairman's Service Award by the Council for Entrepreneurial Development and the Service to Entrepreneurs Award by the Coastal Entrepreneurial Council. He has also been recognized for outstanding service by the U.S. Small Business Administration for establishing and being the Director of UNCW's Small Business Institute for twenty years.

He served on the faculty at Arizona State University where he earned his Ph.D. and as a Visiting Professor of Entrepreneurship in Duke University's Executive MBA program.

He was President of Harper and Associates Inc., a business consulting firm from 1976 through 2009. He has also been the co-founder and President of numerous economic development organizations including: The Coastal Entrepreneurial Council, In-Ventures Inc., and DARE Inc. He has also served on the board of directors for numerous organizations.

He has conducted hundreds of seminars on strategic thinking, breakthrough leadership, corporate entrepreneurship, and the management of change for corporations, not-for-profit enterprises, and government agencies at the national, state, and municipal levels in the United States and Canada. He has also made presentations to more than one hundred professional associations and been a speaker for Inc. Resources.

Foreword

I must ask you, "Why did you decide to read this book? Are you one of us crazies, looking for a cure? Or do you just want to know what makes us different?"

Some of the answers are found in the following chapters of Dr. Stephen Harper's latest book on entrepreneurship, *Here's to the Crazy Entrepreneurs.*

Dr. Harper has spent his twenty-five plus year career as a professor of entrepreneurship studying entrepreneurs and is the author of several acclaimed books on the subject. Most importantly, during his career, Dr. Harper has been a mentor, promoter, guide and friend of many budding and established entrepreneurs.

So, here we go …………

Since recognizing my own propensity for craziness, I have discovered that:

1. Psychiatry has not yet classified a syndrome for us crazies.
2. A 10 step program has not been developed for our recovery.
3. There are no Anonymous programs for us to join.
4. BANKRUPTCY IS THE ONE-STOP SHOP.
5. No help group exists to comfort us as most people, even those in business, do not understand us and the way our brains operate.

My first indication that I was "one of us crazies" was when I was sitting in a college chemistry class writing a business plan for my first business venture which, fortunately, was successful.

Most of us did not start on this path by design or willingly. ... It just happened.

The affliction is worldwide. Via an industry association, I have had the opportunity to visit over 60 countries around the globe. During these trips, I have met and traded stories with many of my crazy compatriots.

Probably the best proof there exists an RNA sequence on a chromosome is the explosion of entrepreneurship in the formerly communist countries. In these countries, there are no mentors, pathways, business plans to copy or business schools to attend.

I have had the pleasure of lecturing to Dr. Harper's seniors many times on the subject of the "Dark side of entrepreneurship" and what it really means to live this path.

So join me in exploring *Here's to the Crazy Entrepreneurs* as Dr. Harper discovers what it is that really makes us crazy.

Robert S. Rippy has been involved in numerous business ventures - including startups and acquisitions. He has also been a franchisee. He has held leadership positions in numerous organizations - including serving as Chairman of the International Association of Amusement Parks and Attractions and serving on the Board of Governors for the University of North Carolina system.

Preface

This book *officially* began at 1:20 p.m. on April 27th, 2012. I remember the moment because I was meeting with the judges for our Annual Business Plan Competition. We had finished our discussion a few minutes earlier than expected about the protocol and criteria for evaluating the students who were about to present their business plans so I asked the judges who are or have been entrepreneurs to share their thoughts about two potential covers for my new book, *Taking Your Business to the Next Level and Beyond.*

When one of the judges asked if I had any plans for another book, I noted that I have been fortunate to have had all the articles I have ever written published in academic and practitioner journals – except one. When they asked about "the one" I noted that my article about whether entrepreneurism is a mental disorder had not been published. Their response was like a chorus. They exclaimed, "Of course it is."

That was the "1:20 p.m. epiphany." I noted that I had submitted the article to numerous respected journals, but that the editors had turned it down for various reasons. The reasons included it was not scholarly enough, it did not have a sufficient empirical base, it did not have enough statistics to analyze, and so forth. The closest it came to being accepted for publication was when the editor of a highly respected university journal said she really liked the article but because she had just taken over as the editor she did not have, as she put it, "the courage to publish it." She noted that the advisory board wanted to elevate the scholarly nature of the journal and that is just wasn't scholarly enough.

At that time I activated my defense mechanisms that humans use to deal with unpleasant realities. First I activated my "What do they know about the subject?" defense mechanism. I knew from the day I started writing the article that only entrepreneurs truly understand entrepreneurs. Therefore, how could a person in an academic environment understand the true nature of entrepreneurs? Most academics operate in an alternate universe from where entrepreneurs do their thing.

Second, I activated the "A lot of truly successful people were turned down numerous times before someone recognized the value of their ideas, products, services, and so forth" defense mechanism. I had heard stories about how George Lucas's idea for the film *Star Wars* had been turned down by numerous studios. I had heard stories about how J.K. Rowling had her manuscript for a book about a young wizard rejected by numerous publishing houses. I had heard about Sarah Blakely being turned down by numerous mills when she approached them about making Spanx. I had also heard stories about how the Beatles were turned down by a recording studio executive who stated something along the lines of "Groups with guitars are on their way out."

By now you can see there are a lot of opportunities to blame the world for not seeing what you think has considerable value. The "What do they know?" defense mechanism can be a very effective way to deal with the agony of defeat and to persist in your quest.

The 1:20 p.m. chorus was the tipping point. Steve Jobs was known to say, "You have to drive the stake in the ground." when he wanted to make things happen. At 1:20 p.m. I decided to drive a stake in the ground and write this book.

Fortunately, I was able to focus on orchestrating the business plan competition that afternoon and to recognize the four students who presented interesting business concepts and corresponding business plans. Their enthusiasm and ability to identify market opportunities were heartening because they showed the entrepreneurial dream is alive and well.

When I went to bed that evening I was looking forward to recharging my batteries after what had been a very busy week. A long and refreshing sleep, however, was not to be the case. When I am writing, my subconscious mind constantly attacks my conscious mind. It is very similar to when entrepreneurs sense an opportunity. Just as they have difficulty focusing on their regular activities - including eating and sleeping when they are sensing and seizing opportunities, my brain kept spitting out idea after idea throughout the night and into the hours before dawn.

I have learned over the years not to try to remember an idea that comes in the dark of night and to write it down after I get up in the morning. Instead, I find it far more helpful to write it down on a Post-it note®. I realized years ago I could not articulate some of the ideas in the morning if I did not write them down when they were fresh in my mind. In the early hours of April 28th my mind was like a popcorn popper. I would come up with an idea for the book, get up and write it down, go back to bed, and try to sleep only to find that another cornel of an idea would pop and set the same set of events in motion.

After the popper kept popping for over an hour I decided to surrender and get up when I came up with another idea. When I got to the vanity in the bathroom, where I had placed my Post-it® notes, I encountered more than thirty of the yellow sheets stuck around the sink. By the way, the bathroom is closer to my bed than my office, so I placed them there rather than run the risk of losing my thoughts. I have also found that I need to turn the light on so I can write legibly – which means I cannot turn on my bedside light without jeopardizing my marriage. My wife already knows I am not "all right in my head," but why risk splitting half my royalties with her in a divorce if I constantly wake her up by turning on the light.

Yet the idea popper kept popping from the darkness of my mind even as I tried to shave, take a shower, and eat breakfast. Each idea would soon be pushed aside by another idea. My mind was in the moment or as athletes say, "in the zone." It could not be deterred or distracted. It was like a hound on a hunt.

The mental disorder idea popper continues even to this day. I might as well wear a t-shirt that says, "I am sorry if it seems like I am not here right now, I am working on a new book." I hope you enjoy this book. I do not know if all the demons that have been popping in my mind have been exorcised by writing this book but at least for now I can say that it is done. Also, I believe this is my last book –

unless the idea popper starts up again. If it does, then I recognize - to use the words from Star Trek,

"Resistance is futile."

Introduction

ENTREPRENEURS ARE NOT LIKE *"NORMAL"* PEOPLE

"It is easy to find fault with a new idea.
It is easier to say it can't be done, than to try.
Thus, it is through the fear of failure,
That some men create their own hell."

E. Jacob Taylor

Normal people cannot understand why entrepreneurs would risk their health, marriages, and mortgages to start businesses. *Normal* people exclaim, "Are you crazy?" when someone announces he/she is thinking about starting a business. *Normal* people cannot understand how people can quit their jobs to do what they and possibly no one else has ever done.

What drives entrepreneurs to live at the edge? Are they missing the risk-aversion gene? Are entrepreneurs the only people who understand entrepreneurs? Why is it that starting a business can be such an obsession? What drives entrepreneurs to start multiple businesses? Do some entrepreneurs have attention deficit disorder? Can the demon that drives their obsessiveness to start businesses be exorcised? Is it impossible to be a "reformed" entrepreneur? This book takes a closer look at whether entrepreneurs have a mental disorder that drives them to do things *normal* people would not even consider doing.

In addition to being an entrepreneur, I have had the pleasure of interacting and working with entrepreneurs in various capacities. My research into what makes entrepreneurs tick includes interviews with over two-hundred entrepreneurs as well as conversations with hundreds of other entrepreneurs.

Three things are clear about people who march to the beat of the entrepreneurial drummer. First, people who start ventures are different from other people. Most people who do not dream of starting a business do not understand why people try to traverse the entrepreneurship minefield. An entrepreneur who started a software firm noted, "My wife just doesn't understand why I would want to start a business." Louis Armstrong Jr. may have captured this man's predicament with his wife and countless others. The great trumpeter observed, "There are some people who don't know and you just can't tell them."

Second, entrepreneurs are as multi-faceted as a diamond. Their varied personalities, perceptions, and backgrounds contribute to their heterogeneity. Certain factors and experiences affect people's propensity to be entrepreneurs. Some entrepreneurs have bigger than life personalities like Richard Branson and Steve Jobs. Other entrepreneurs keep a low profile and do not seek the limelight or celebrity status. Some entrepreneurs seem to approach the world with near-reckless abandon. Other entrepreneurs have varying levels of paranoia that causes them to always be on the lookout for forces that could derail their success. Some entrepreneurs – like Steve Jobs – want to "make a dent in the universe" or disrupt the marketplace by introducing a breakthrough product, service, or technology. Other entrepreneurs just want to bring an existing product, service, or technology to a market that has not experienced it before.

Third, people who start businesses should not be lumped into one species. It would be a mistake to group people into the two undifferentiated categories: non-entrepreneurs and entrepreneurs. Each category can be seen as a continuum. Among the non-entrepreneurs, people who would never dream of starting a business are at one end of the continuum. At the other end of the non-entrepreneur continuum are people who constantly think about starting a business but who will probably never pull the entrepreneurial trigger.

The entrepreneurial group is composed of so many different types of people that they almost defy categorization. The entrepreneurial continuum has people at one end who are committed to starting one or more ventures and who systematically analyze the marketplace for entrepreneurial opportunities. Anthony A. Martino deliberately embarked on the entrepreneurial journey by systematically analyzing the automobile industry for areas where people's needs were not being met well or at all. His search led to the creation of MAACO and AAMCO.

Then there are people who may not have planned to start a business – or at least not at that time. Some people become entrepreneurs by "bumping" into opportunities like Jerry Yang and David Filo as graduate students at Stanford. Jerry Yang and David Filo noticed problems associated with collecting information on the Internet. Their realization prompted them to create Yahoo! even though it may not have been on their career "to do" lists. A few years later, Sergey Brin and Larry Page, who also were graduate students at Stanford, became entrepreneurs even though that may not have been their plan. Their effort to improve search engines and their desire to have search ratings based on actual searches rather than paid placements put them in a position where investors approached them to become entrepreneurs to start Google.

Two particular types of entrepreneurs stand out when it comes to "being driven" to start businesses. They are like moths driven to an open flame. They are the entrepreneurs who start multiple ventures: serial entrepreneurs and multipreneurs. These two groups of entrepreneurs tend to operate with a very different mindset than most entrepreneurs.

Serial entrepreneurs do not settle for starting and staying with just one venture. Their lives are like a relay race. They start one venture then sell it or have someone take the helm so they can start another venture. Their lives are like a book with many chapters with each chapter being a startup. Multipreneurs are different from serial entrepreneurs because they start and run numerous ventures in a concurrent rather than sequential manner.

Richard Branson may be the ultimate multipreneur. He has started hundreds of ventures. His "Virgin" empire currently includes over two hundred businesses. His contempt for businesses and industries that are complacent has led him to start ventures that offer what existing businesses fail to offer. Richard Branson's ventures include a broad variety of businesses including a railroad, an airline, a cell phone service, and numerous retail establishments.

This book takes a closer look at what drives entrepreneurs. It also profiles various maladies to answer the question, "Is entrepreneurism a mental disorder?" The reader, however, should be cautioned before reading on. If you are an entrepreneur or contemplating becoming an entrepreneur, you may find that you are, in fact, one of the crazy ones.

In 1997 Steve Jobs worked with advertising agency TBWA\Chiat\Day to capture the spirit that drives Apple to do great things. Their *"Think Different"* message continues to have a profound impact on people. I have known people who have changed jobs, started businesses, had their entrepreneurial spirit reenergized, and changed their lives in other ways after watching the video and seeing how Steve Jobs incorporates it into his 2005 commencement address at Stanford which can be found on YouTube. It is a "must see."

"Think Different" is such an important part of this book's message that readers are encouraged to check out Richard Dreyfuss reciting it on YouTube and to see the pictures Steve Jobs chose to go with it. The *Think Different* ad can be seen at the following YouTube site. It is definitely work a look. It played an instrumental role in my decision to write this book. The YouTube site at the time is: http://www.youtube.com/watch?v=D9T_5MeFA1M

Chapter One

A CLOSER LOOK: WHAT MAKES ENTREPRENEURS TICK?

*"A lot of people have ideas and see opportunities, but few have
the courage and persistence to see them through.
A lot of people have dreams, but few have the ability
to transform them into viable businesses."*
Stephen C. Harper

For every person who starts a business, there are probably ten people who are thinking about starting one. Some people start "lifestyle" businesses. They start a business merely as an alternative to having a job. Some people start businesses that really did not plan to start businesses. Some people start businesses after they have been laid off. These people have been labeled "reluctant entrepreneurs." Some people stumble into an opportunity through their work or personal lives that drives them to start a business. Some people know they want to start their own businesses *sometime* in their lives. This is the "someday" group. They are just waiting for the right opportunity and the right set of personal circumstances. They hope they will be in a position to quit their jobs and pursue their entrepreneurial dream. Some of these people wait and wait … and never become entrepreneurs.

Then there are the people who are *driven* to embark on the entrepreneurial journey. They do not wait for the "perfect" opportunity, nor do they wait for all their stars to be perfectly aligned. For them, entrepreneurship is not a career choice; it is a calling. For them, life is too short to sit on the sidelines waiting for a turn to play.

To the *driven ones*, being a spectator is not an option. They are compelled to seize the day.

While entrepreneurship refers to the process for starting a business; entrepreneurism can be viewed as a *mindset*. Entrepreneurism reflects how entrepreneurs see the world around them, their desire to be their own boss, and their attitude about risk. Certain factors and experiences affect one's propensity to be an entrepreneur. There has been a running discussion about whether entrepreneurs are born or made – whether they are determined by their DNA or whether they are a product of their experiences and environment. This book does not try to settle the "nature vs. nurture" debate. Instead, it recognizes that entrepreneurism is the product of numerous factors including one's experiences while growing up and during one's career. It recognizes that entrepreneurism is affected by one's personality and perceptions as well as market conditions.

The Nature of "Real" Entrepreneurs

Years ago, Peter Drucker drew the distinction between people who start businesses and real entrepreneurs. Peter Drucker was considered one of the great business thinkers of the 20th Century. He noted while a lot of people *start* businesses, real entrepreneurs *bring something "new"* to the marketplace. I agree with Peter Drucker's distinction. Simply starting a business that is no different from another business down the block or in another zip code does not make a person a *real* entrepreneur.

This book is about *real* entrepreneurs. The entrepreneurial badge of courage can only be worn by people who take the risk associated with starting a venture that brings something *new* to the marketplace. People who start businesses that are like other businesses take a risk because they are *not very different* from existing businesses in their market space. They, in fact, may be crazier than real entrepreneurs.

Even though I have been interacting with fellow entrepreneurs for over forty years, I am still amazed at how entrepreneurism is viewed so differently by the people who embark on the entrepreneurial journey and the people who wonder why anyone would deliberately put themselves in harm's way. I am also amazed that researchers who are not entrepreneurs try to find out what makes entrepreneurs tick. Some of their research has actually debunked some entrepreneurial misconceptions and myths. Other research efforts, however, have been almost comical. One study even analyzed similarities between entrepreneurs and social workers. Really!

When I was writing my first book on entrepreneurship, my editor asked me to develop an entrepreneurial quiz. I told him that if people needed to take a test to see if they are entrepreneurial, then they should not waste their time … they are not entrepreneurial.

This book also draws the distinction between people who are driven by their desire to seize an opportunity – rather than those who "back into" entrepreneurship as a result of losing their jobs. Real entrepreneurs do not see being an entrepreneur as one of the alternatives in a multiple choice career question. Real entrepreneurs do not see having a regular job in an established firm as an option. This book also differentiates real entrepreneurs from what some people call "reluctant entrepreneurs," who are people who lost their jobs and start a business to pay for their mortgage and other financial obligations. Real entrepreneurs do not *back into* being an entrepreneur. Starting ventures is who they are and what they do.

This book also makes the distinction between three other types of people who are often referred to as entrepreneurs. Corporate entrepreneurs are the first group. While they may be very innovative and launch new products and services, they are not real entrepreneurs because the firms they work for provide them with a safety net. Even though they may be launching a new initiative, they usually have facilities, funding, and support services at their disposal, which reduce their risks dramatically. They are also different from real entrepreneurs because they rarely have to mortgage their homes to launch their initiatives. More often than not, they will still have a job if their initiatives do not fulfill expectations. Real entrepreneurs have "skin in the game." If their ventures do not succeed, then they take a significant financial hit. This author respects corporate entrepreneurs – or what Gifford Pinchot III called "intrapreneurs." I just do not consider them to be real entrepreneurs.

It should be noted here, however, that many frustrated corporate entrepreneurs start their own ventures when they get fed up with their employer's bureaucratic barriers, sloth-like pace, and the "We're not in that business" mentality. Their sense of urgency to seize the moment as well as their vision for a better type of business and/or way of doing business often causes them to start their own ventures. Many of today's firms were started by frustrated employees. It is ironic that some of those firm's competitors were started by ticked off employees who sensed opportunities but were discouraged from seizing them.

This book also draws the distinction between social entrepreneurs and real entrepreneurs. While the people who start non-profit enterprises to address social ills should be revered they, like corporate entrepreneurs, rarely mortgage their homes to launch their organizations. They too may have the passion to make things happen, but not risking all they have to start the venture separates them from real entrepreneurs.

The last group is composed of "enterprising" individuals. They are often called entrepreneurs because they make things happen by buying other businesses and by adding other firms' products and/or territories to their own firms. In a few cases, enterprising individuals may be seen as real entrepreneurs. If they got involved in a venture in its formative years and completely transformed it via their vision, passion, innovativeness, and perseverance, then they may be real entrepreneurs. Tony Hsieh and Howard Schultz may be in this category. Tony Hsieh may not have started Zappos, but he transformed it into one of the most successful brands in the United States. Howard Schultz did not start Starbucks, but he transformed it from a retail store that sold coffee "beans" into a multi-dimensional business that spans the globe.

Cautionary Note: Each of the following characteristics of real entrepreneurs needs to be seen from a situational perspective. While these characteristics can be very beneficial, they can be detrimental if taken to an extreme. This is why each characteristic will be followed by a "cautionary note" that profiles the potential threats and consequences of each characteristic if it is totally unbridled. The *Dr. Jekyll and Mr. Hyde* nature of the characteristics will be discussed in more depth later in this book. In this case, Dr. Jekyll will refer to constructive behavior. Mr. Hyde will refer to behavior that may so extreme that it has negative consequences.

Real Entrepreneurs Are Driven

What causes people to boldly go where they and possibly no one has gone before? What causes them to be the Davids who challenge the Goliaths and other firms? What drives them to challenge the status quo, to quit their jobs, or to drop out of school to start ventures? What causes them to risk their marriages, mortgages, health, and alienation from their kids and pets? Are they like moths driven to a flame? Are they missing the risk-aversion gene? Why are they not like *normal* people who work within the system?

The tendency for real entrepreneurs to "step into darkness" is captured in the following passage from Theodore Roosevelt's "Citizenship in a Republic" speech at the Sorbonne in Paris on April 23, 1910.

> *"It is not the critic who counts:*
> *not the man who points out how the strong*
> *man stumbles or where the doer of deeds could have done better.*
> *The credit belongs to the man who is actually in the arena,*
> *whose face is marred by dust and sweat and blood,*
> *who strives valiantly, who errs and comes up short again and again,*
> *because there is no effort without error or shortcoming,*
> *but who knows the great enthusiasms, the great devotions,*
> *who spends himself for a worthy cause; who, at the best, knows,*
> *in the end, the triumph of high achievement, and who,*
> *at the worst, if he fails, at least he fails while daring greatly,*
> *so that his place shall never be with those cold and timid souls*
> *who knew neither victory nor defeat."*

Real entrepreneurs recognize that success is rarely assured and that failure is almost inevitable somewhere along the way in their entrepreneurial journey. Most entrepreneurs will acknowledge that if you have never failed, then you did not set your goals high enough or try to break new ground.

Daniel Isenberg, a professor at Babson College, made four interesting observations about fear and failure in his *Harvard Business Review* article, "Entrepreneurs and the Cult of Failure." First, he noted that policy makers for numerous governments around the world are advocating "embracing failure" to encourage entrepreneurship. Second, he noted that entrepreneurs develop a healthy fear of what can go wrong, but they don't let it paralyze them. Third, failure is a natural part of doing business. Fourth, failures are important because they foster learning.[1]

A few years ago, Jim Collins - the author of numerous bestselling books on leadership - wrote an article for *Fast Company* about the challenges associated with mountain climbing. He noted that to not stretch to your limits is to fail. He noted that when you truly give something your best efforts and do not succeed in that effort, it is not a failure. Collins calls such an effort a "fallure."

Mountain climbing may be a bit extreme for most people to relate to. Snow skiing, however, may provide a better example of how real entrepreneurs view fallure. The best skiers became the best because they fell and they fell often. They fell because they were trying to increase their ability and to master the slopes. They recognized they grow only when they try to do things they have never done. They got better with each fall because they learned from their falls and adjusted their approach. They also knew the difference between stretching and being reckless. They learned from their falls and grew by taking on more challenging slopes rather than starting the sport on steep and bumpy black diamond runs. People who are afraid of falling and planting their faces in the snow – or even getting cold – rarely ascend the slopes. People who accept that skiing involves falling have the opportunity to experience the joy of skiing.

Real entrepreneurs agree with Jim Collins' distinction between failure and fallure. They recognize that *not* making the effort to seize an opportunity is a much greater loss than to have made the effort and not succeeded. They share Alfred Tennyson's words from part of his 1850 poem "*In Memoriam*" stanza *XXVII*.

> *"I hold it true, whate'er befall;*
> *I feel it, when I sorrow most;*

'Tis better to have loved and lost
Than never to have loved at all."

Savvy entrepreneurs, thereby, see the risk of failure in a different way than *normal* people. When faced with a major challenge, barrier, or setback, savvy entrepreneurs echo Gene Kranz's classic line, "Failure is not an option." When the lives of the Apollo 13 crew were in peril, someone at NASA stated that the situation could be NASA's darkest hour. Gene Kranz noted, however, that if the engineers at NASA could rise to the challenge, it could be NASA's *finest* hour.

Cautionary Note: Being driven may provide a person with considerable persistence to meet a challenge and the resilience needed to get back up when one has been knocked down. Yet unbridled drive can blind a person to reality. While a lot of entrepreneurs relish the opportunity to make the impossible possible, there will be times when "willing it" will not make it so. The exclamation, "never give up" can be very motivating, but there will be times when it is best to move on and invest your energy, ideas, and resources in something else.

Real Entrepreneurs Live at the Edge

Successful entrepreneurs have been heralded for being visionaries and having the courage to put everything on the line to start their ventures. Their boldness, irreverence, decisiveness, impatience, persistence, passion, hustle, and so forth have been glorified by the media. Real entrepreneurs seem to thrive when they are at the edge. Karl Wallenda, the great tightrope aerialist, captured the thrill associated with operating at "the entrepreneurial edge." When he was asked what it was like to be so far above the ground without a net he responded, "Life is on the wire, the rest is just waiting."

To real entrepreneurs, starting a business is being on the tightrope; everything else is waiting. They cannot imagine another vocation that provides the adrenalin rush. It is ironic that after Karl Wallenda fell to his death, his wife noted he seemed preoccupied with the prospect of falling rather than succeeding that day. Can the fear of failure be a self-fulfilling prophecy?

Cautionary Note: The issue of work-life balance has recently gained considerable attention. The notion of "balance" and mental health will be discussed later in this book. The adrenalin rush of being on the wire can be addictive, but people need to take time out periodically to recharge their batteries. If not, then they can be like a light bulb that is its brightest just before it loses its illumination.

Real Entrepreneurs Embrace Uncertainty, Ambiguity, and Risk

Times of rapid change are times of turbulence and ambiguity. Most people are like deer that are frozen in the headlights of an oncoming truck. The greater the change, the more normal people freeze and reminisce about the good old days.

The U.S. Small Business Administration estimates that about one-third of all Americans between the ages of 20 and 65 are thinking about starting a business. That's more than 50 million people. Yet only 1 million businesses are started each year. Many of these businesses are started by people who have already started at least one venture. This means that less than two percent of the people who are thinking about starting a business will actually start one this year. This demonstrates that the fear of failure may be stronger than the fear of missing an opportunity.

The whole notion of starting a venture creates anxiety for most people. Entrepreneurship involves "stepping into darkness." Henry David Thoreau captured the tendency for most people to not step forward to seize the moment in his book *Walden.* He noted, "The mass of men lead lives of quiet desperation."

Real entrepreneurs exhibit a "Bring it on" attitude. While they may not know what they will encounter in starting a business, they are confident they can handle the challenges. Brett Martin, Founder of Castle Branch Inc., is grateful entrepreneurship has so many challenges and risks. He notes, "If entrepreneurship was easy, then everyone would be an entrepreneur." To him, the challenges and risks serve as barriers that keep people out that are not committed enough to accept the risks and challenges.

Entrepreneurship involves sensing and seizing opportunities. Winston Churchill captured the notion of opportunity loss and regret minimization when he stated, "To every man there comes in his lifetime that special moment when he is figuratively tapped on the shoulder and offered that chance to do a very special thing, unique to him and fitted to his talent. What a tragedy if that moment finds him unprepared or unqualified for the work that could have been his finest hour."

Yet starting a business may not be that big of a risk to savvy entrepreneurs. They make every effort to start the venture off on the right foot. They position themselves and their ventures to mitigate risk because:

- They put together a qualified management team to reduce the number of mistakes.
- They come in with sufficient funding to get their ventures to the point where they can generate a positive cash flow.
- They also have sufficient funding in reserve to deal with the inevitable surprises and setbacks.
- They do enough market research to determine where there are frustrated people in search of a business that will solve their problems and what it will take to convert them into customers.
- They try to have committed customers lined up – possibly with purchase orders – before the business opens so they have a solid revenue stream from the start.
- They get the necessary permits, licenses, and contracts ironed out in advance.
- They have a proprietary position that will provide them with a sustainable competitive advantage.
- They launch in a forgiving marketplace.
- They also have allies and board members who can provide valuable advice, open important doors and accelerate growth.

Entrepreneurial risk is truly in the eyes of the beholder. Life can be seen as a series of decisions that are based on perceived risks and consequences. Each person has a threshold for risk. If the perceived probability of failure is low, then the person may proceed. If the perceived consequences of failure are low, then the person may proceed. If both are low, then there will be little hesitance. Michael Dell started his computer business while he was a freshman at the University of Texas. He did not consider his computer venture to be much of a risk because if it failed he could just stay in school.

When Jeff Bezos recognized the e-commerce wave was forming, he could not resist it. He quit his job on Wall Street to capture some of the e-commerce wave. When asked how he could take such a risk he stated that he believed the industry was at a "critical category formation time."[2]

Jeff Bezos' motivation to start Amazon.com reflects how the fear of missing an opportunity can be a driving force. He noted in a *60 Minutes* interview in Amazon's early years that he lives his life with a "regret minimization framework."[3] He translated his philosophy into something along the lines that when he looks back and reflects on his life, he wants to have the least amount of regrets. If he had not quit his job in New York to seize the opportunity to ride the e-commerce tsunami, then he would certainly have regretted missing it.

Chris Argyris, as a psychologist, provided an interesting and useful distinction between two types of anxieties.[4] He noted Anxiety I occurs when people think about all the things that could go wrong and the corresponding consequences. People experiencing a high level of Anxiety I tend to avoid situations that produce it. In the entrepreneurial context, their fear of losing money, their esteem, and so forth keep them from taking the entrepreneurial journey.

Anxiety II is quite different from Anxiety I. It is associated with the risks and consequences of *not doing* something. In the entrepreneurial context, it reflects Jeff Bezos's concern about missing the opportunity to start a business to capitalize on the incredible opportunities that would come with the increase in e-commerce.

The anxiety associated with missing an opportunity can be so strong that it interferes with everything people do who sense untapped opportunities. They can't eat, drink, sleep, or do their jobs because they are thinking about a specific opportunity, and how they cannot let it pass them by. The preoccupation with the opportunity and the anxiety associated with not missing it can be so strong that it becomes an obsession. If Anxiety II for a person is stronger than Anxiety I, then he/she may embark on the entrepreneurial journey.

Cautionary Note: There are situations where the level of risk may be excessive. Years ago, Richard Branson hosted the show, *The Rebel Billionaire: Branson's Quest for the Best* that was similar in concept to Donald Trump's *The Apprentice*. One of the points made by Richard Branson - who is one of the world's greatest thrill seekers - was that there is a line where the risks associated with some activities far exceed the potential rewards - and that knowing the difference between taking calculated risks and being reckless is crucial for entrepreneurs.

Real Entrepreneurs are Opportunistic, Decisive, and Committed

Real entrepreneurs will not rest until the targeted opportunity is seized. They are not perfectionists because they recognize that perfectionists never do anything that has risk. This is why accountants, engineers, and others who are taught not to make judgment calls are rarely willing to "step into the darkness" that is part of starting a venture.

Real entrepreneurs do not succumb to paralysis by analysis because they know the market does not wait for those who try to avert risk by studying things to death. They know when you are at the edge you do not have the luxury of having gigabytes of data. They know those who operate with a "ready, aim, aim, aim mentality" rarely pull the trigger. Yet they also know that entrepreneurship requires more than flying by the seat of your pants. They recognize that making "educated" judgment calls is an essential part of starting and running a business. Nicholas Murray Butler captured how people are different when he stated:

"People can be divided into three groups:
People who make things happen, those who watch things happen,
and those that wonder what happened."

Real entrepreneurs know windows of opportunity open and close quickly in times of change. They have a "launch and learn" mentality. They know the best way to learn about how the market will respond to their innovative products, services, and business models is to get them into the hands of potential customers as soon as possible. They know the speed in launching market trials and the ability to quickly modify and re-launch their offerings after learning what the market does and does not value can give their firms a competitive edge.

Two Chinese proverbs capture how real entrepreneurs see opportunities when others see darkness. The first proverb, "When the wind of change blows some build walls while others build windmills." captures the difference between normal people and real entrepreneurs. Normal people are often the spectators of change. Entrepreneurs seize the opportunity by initiating the change.

The second proverb, "A time of crisis is also a time of opportunity." captures how real entrepreneurs welcome discontinuities. This proverb has evolved into a more modern saying, "It would be a shame to not capitalize on a crisis." Real entrepreneurs recognize how they approach change will determine if they will be the beneficiaries of change or the casualties of change. They know that the best way to be a beneficiary is to be the initiator of the change. Real entrepreneurs agree with Alan Kay's philosophy about how to deal with change. Alan Kay who was an Apple Fellow noted, "The best way to predict the future is to invent it."

Real entrepreneurs relish challenges. Entrepreneurship involves identifying questions (problems or gaps) in the market place and then coming up with the solutions. Steve Jobs was known for starting meetings by placing "What is the question?" on the flip chart. Real entrepreneurs, like Steve Jobs, believe that just because something has never been done doesn't mean it can't be done. They also believe that just because they may not have done something does not mean they cannot do it. A lot of their success can be attributed to their perceptiveness, mentality dexterity, innovative spirit, and resourcefulness. If there isn't an answer to the question, then they will create one. Real entrepreneurs approach the world with a similar attitude that Phil Knight had when Nike developed the motto "*Just do it*." Real entrepreneurs have a "*Just try it*" mentality.

Two very different people captured the proactive nature of entrepreneurism. George Bernard Shaw observed, "The people who get on in this world are the people who get up and look for what they want, and if they can't find it, make them." Dr. Ing. h.c. F. Porsche AG noted, "You must have the freedom to look beyond what has been done before ... I couldn't find the car I dreamed of, so I decided to build it myself."

Some entrepreneurs have made an effort to delete the word "problem" from their vocabulary. The word "problem" has a negative connotation to many people. While Steve Jobs focused on solving problems, most *normal* people want to avoid or even rationalize away "problems."

Some proactive entrepreneurs have replaced the word problem with "situation." Situation has a more neutral tone to it. You do not hear about people in the White House meeting in the *problem* room; they meet in the *Situation* Room. Yet in the world of entrepreneurs, the word *situation* is too neutral; the word *challenge* is far more appropriate. Which type of meeting would you rather be in? - one that starts with someone asking "What types of problems are we facing?" or one that starts with "What challenges are we facing that will give us the opportunity to excel?"

Most angel investors and venture capital firms consider the ability of the entrepreneur to make the right decisions to be more important than the quality of the opportunity being pursued. They prefer to bet on "A" entrepreneurs (and their teams) who are pursuing "B" opportunities more than "B" entrepreneurs pursuing "A" opportunities. Their bet is based on the belief that "A" entrepreneurs can make the best out of opportunities - even "B" opportunities. They do not have the same level of faith in the ability of "B" entrepreneurs to make the right decisions – even if they are pursuing "A" opportunities.

Decisiveness plays an integral role in entrepreneurism. Real entrepreneurs know there is a time to think, a time to analyze, a time to decide, a time to plan the implementation of your decision, and the time to implement the decision. The process and risks associated with starting a venture keep entrepreneurial wannabes on the sidelines.

Real entrepreneurs are not spectators. They savor and seize the moment. They turn adversity, problems, and gaps in the marketplace into new venture opportunities. They know that while knowledge is power; they also know they will never have complete, accurate, and timely information. Real entrepreneurs recognize - to use the phrase from *Star Trek* - nothing really happens until you "engage the warp drive." They know that he who hesitates loses to those who recognize that time is of the essence and engage the warp drive.

Cautionary Note: One of the prerequisites for success is knowing what you don't know - especially as it pertains to yourself. All entrepreneurs have shortcomings they may not be aware of and blind spots that keep them from seeing certain things. The saying, "What you don't know can kill you." applies here. This is why it is so important for entrepreneurs to surround themselves with people who are smarter than them and who are candid when they see the entrepreneur is either unaware of something or ignoring it altogether. Andrew Grove, while leading Intel, valued the people on his staff who challenged his assumptions by playing the role of the Devil's Advocate. He called them "Helpful Cassandras."

Real Entrepreneurs are Unconventional and Irreverent

It was not that long ago that entrepreneurs were considered mavericks and in some cases, social outcasts. Most entrepreneurs were considered "unemployable" because they could not and would not "fit in." Things have certainly changed. It was not that long ago that people were heralded for being *company men*. Now, some of the entrepreneurs who *march to the beat of a different drummer* have gained celebrity status as entrepreneurial icons – a space that had been reserved for rock stars and exceptional athletes. Their ability to change, break, or even ignore the rules have also made them millionaires and, in some cases, billionaires.

Real entrepreneurs look at the world through different lenses. They look for things others don't look for. They see things others don't see. They think thoughts others don't think. They do things that others won't do. When Steve Jobs returned to Apple, he created an environment where people could think differently again. This atmosphere helped foster Apple's Renaissance.

Real entrepreneurs are not conformists. They do not show reverence for authority or the way things are done. They don't think or operate "within the box." They do not "color within the lines." They have contempt for the status quo and challenge conventional wisdom. They don't follow the rules if they don't make sense or if they are applied to situations that do not fit new realities.

Real entrepreneurs relish the opportunity to change the way the game is played and look for markets where established firms are no longer in sync with consumer expectations. They particularly enjoy the prospect of creative destruction. They seek avenues for developing killer applications that blow established products, services, processes, and/or businesses out of the market.

Real entrepreneurs not only create new products, services and processes; they create new business models and industries. They also transform industries. Howard Head demonstrated the ability shake up the tennis industry and ski industry when he questioned why products had to be made of wood. He recognized that wood was fairly brittle and subject to warping. He revolutionized both industries by developing and offering metal skis and tennis rackets.

Cautionary Note: Numerous entrepreneurs make the mistake of thinking success is contingent on being different. Being different does not assure success. Success in the marketplace involves being better – and to be better you have to be different in ways the market values and is willing to pay for. Years ago an inventor created and patented panty hose with three legs. He considered his panty hose to be better because if one leg got a run in it, then that leg could be rolled up and the spare leg could be rolled down so the woman could continue with her activities. This is a case where different is not necessarily better. Entrepreneurs need to recognize *better* is defined by the marketplace, not them.

Real Entrepreneurs are Driven to Solve Problems

Someone once noted that within every problem lies at least one disguised business opportunity. Real entrepreneurs thrive on finding solutions to problems in the marketplace. Every time they hear, "I wish there was a way to …" they light up. Even if they initially do not have a way to solve the problem, they will find a way for it to be solved. Here is one of the distinctions between inventors and entrepreneurs. Inventors are driven to *develop* the solution; entrepreneurs are driven to *find* and offer the solution – even if they have to buy it, license it, or hire people to develop it. A lot of entrepreneurs are like systems integrators. They take different resources (people, technology, information, and so forth) and bring them together to bring value to the marketplace.

When a very successful information technology entrepreneur was asked about his formula for success, he stated, "ten percent inspiration and ninety percent theft." When he was challenged on the theft part of the formula, he clarified it by stating that theft involves taking ideas that exist in one setting and applying them to a different situation and/or in a different way. Ironically, marketing theorists consider such a practice to be a legitimate form of innovation. They call it "selective imitation."

People often ask me to describe the differences between real entrepreneurs and executives in established firms. I note that executives are like joggers who like running on established roadways. Real entrepreneurs like running through uncharted territory with an uneven terrain. Most joggers (executives) like to measure their time and distance (sales, profits, market share). Most runners (entrepreneurs), however, live in the moment as they encounter each challenge (problem to be solved or opportunity to be seized) the terrain brings. Their "high" does not come from jogging – it comes from jumping over creeks, avoiding tree roots, dodging branches, and hurdling downed limbs. Joggers - especially distance runners - welcome their *second wind*. Runners, however, have a *continuous adrenalin rush* because they see the string of obstacles they face as challenges.

Cautionary Note: Entrepreneurs like to consider themselves to be "solution providers." Yet they need to make sure the marketplace will buy their solutions. 3M applies a three-question screen when it reviews proposals for developing new products. Proposals must get a yes to the following questions: "Can we make it?", "Will they buy it?", and "Can we make 3M margin with it?" These three questions provide a constructive "reality check." Entrepreneurs need to make sure they don't waste their time and valuable resources on developing a solution for a problem that does not exist or that is too small to justify the investment.

Real Entrepreneurs Have a Keen Sense of Timing

Real entrepreneurs know that knowing *when* to do something can be as important as *what they* plan to do. They know that timing can be the difference between being an outstanding success or a total failure. They know that if their offering hits the market way before the window of opportunity opens, they may die on the vine and/or give their competitors time to develop their own offering. They know that if their offering hits the market after the window has opened, they may be fighting for the table scraps left by the firms that synchronized their offerings to the window opening.

Real entrepreneurs practice "anticipatory management." They demonstrate what is known as the "Gretzky" approach to doing things. As the story goes, when Wayne Gretzky – the great hockey player – was asked to explain why he was so successful, he responded, "A good hockey player plays where the puck is. A great hockey player plays where the puck is going to be."

Instead of focusing all their attention and resources on today, real entrepreneurs focus some of their attention on "what's next and what's after that?" They focus on where the market is heading, rather than just where it is today. They look for trends, leading indicators, run "what if?" scenarios, identify possible discontinuities, and develop contingency plans. They know the value of having resources in reserve to capitalize on unexpected opportunities. They also have resources in reserve to address surprises and the inevitable bumps in the road.

Most people who are responsible for making decisions direct their attention to coming up with the answers to their current questions. More perceptive people try to anticipate the questions so they have time to come up with good answers. Real entrepreneurs go one step further. They come up with the right answers before others have even identified the questions.

By asking the right questions and anticipating where the market is headed, real entrepreneurs anticipate opportunities before others do and have the courage to do what no one has done before. They position their ventures to offer what the market wants even before consumers and competitors may realize it. They position their ventures so they have the markets to themselves as first movers when the window of opportunity opens. This gives their ventures a significant edge in the marketplace.

It has been said by numerous sources that Steve Jobs found little value in conventional market research – particularly asking potential customers what they wanted. He noted that you cannot ask people what they want when they cannot imagine what might be possible. He also noted that people were not asking for desktop video editing so they could make their own movies. But when they saw what the iMac could do, they were blown away.

Cautionary Note: Anticipatory management can give the firm an edge, but entrepreneurs need to avoid spending all their time running "What if?" scenarios for two reasons. First, it is difficult to predict the future. All you can do is try to identify various possible futures and prepare for them. Alvin Toffler noted in his classic book *Future Shock* years ago, that the future has a habit of invading the present. His observation applies even more today with change happening even faster and on even more fronts. The risk here is that the entrepreneur believes he/she sees the future and commits significant resources to his/her version of the future. If that version of the future is off base, then the firm will have committed resources that are no longer available for a future that is different from what was expected. Second, if you spend all your time pondering what the future may hold, then you will be taking your eyes off of your current markets, customers, and operations. As someone noted, "If you don't manage your short term, you will not have a long term." The point to be made in this cautionary note is the same for all the characteristics. Success arises from balance; not the extremes.

Real Entrepreneurs Have the Courage to be Path Makers

The question is often raised, "What role does courage play in entrepreneurship?" Webster's Dictionary defines courage as "the absence of fear." Yet real courage involves overcoming the fear. Real entrepreneurs recognize there are risks, but they do not let the risks keep them from going forward. To them, the consequences of not seizing the moment are greater than the consequences associated with what could happen by trying to seize the moment.

Two terms capture the propensity for entrepreneurs to boldly go where no one has gone before. The first is *stepping into darkness*. Real entrepreneurs are like explorers. They know that when you explore new terrain, you do not have the benefit of a map. They know they have to be path makers, not path takers. They are not taking the road *less traveled*; they are creating the path *to be traveled* through virgin territory – territory that could be full of all sorts of surprises and hazards.

The second term is *taking a leap of faith*. Like Christopher Columbus who believed there had to be a Western path to India – real entrepreneurs have the courage of their convictions. They may not be able to prove to others that an opportunity exists or that they can develop a revolutionary solution to a market problem, but they are willing to move forward while others wait for more tangible evidence.

Ironically, the lack of tangible evidence is what gives entrepreneurs a first-mover advantage. Their ability to envision what may be possible is often sufficient for them to move forward. Whether you call it having the courage of your convictions or having the guts to do something you and possibly no one else has done, it usually involves getting out of your comfort zone. Their ability to free themselves from their comfort zones enables them to be the initiators and beneficiaries of change rather than the spectators and/or casualties of change.

One of the best examples of how entrepreneurs have the courage to leave their comfort zones involves Steven Spielberg. He noted in an interview on *CBS Sunday Morning*[5] that he has Norman Rockwell's 1947 painting *Boy on High Dive* in his office at Amblin Entertainment. The painting originally appeared on the cover of the *Saturday Evening Post* magazine. The painting captures the anxiety and fear of a boy as he contemplates the challenge of jumping off the high dive.

When he was asked if it were his favorite Rockwell painting, he said, "Well, let's put it this way. This is the Rockwell that, every time I'm ready to make a movie, every time I'm ready to commit to direct a movie, that's me - that's the feeling in my gut, before I say 'yes' to a picture. Because every movie is like looking off a three-meter diving board, every one."

Steven Spielberg noted, "We're all on diving boards, hundreds of times during our lives. Taking the plunge or pulling back from the abyss … is something that we must face. For me, that painting represents every motion picture just before I commit to directing it -- just that one moment, before I say, "Yes, I'm going to direct that movie."

He also noted that when it came to *Schindler's List*, he clung to the diving board for 11 years before taking the plunge. "That painting spoke to me the second I saw it … [And when I was able to buy it] I said not only is it going in my collection, but it's going in my office so I can look at it every day of my life."

Cautionary Note: The best entrepreneurs know the difference between taking calculated risks and being reckless. Starting a venture, especially an innovative venture, has inherent risks but savvy entrepreneurs take steps to reduce or minimize risks. They also recognize that the only way to eliminate any risk is not to start a business. Entrepreneurs who pride themselves on being bold and who want to show the world how they can change it, often take excessive risks. Their recklessness usually comes back to bite them and the others involved in their ventures.

While some people say the biggest risk is to not take the risk, there are times when the risk/reward ratio is far too lopsided on the risk side. It is at these times that entrepreneurs need to step back and take a path with a better risk/return ratio. Steve Jobs' desire to change the world and make a dent in the universe may provide considerable inspiration to many entrepreneurs, but it should be noted, that he was just one of a few entrepreneurs out of over a million entrepreneurs who was able to do so. Wise entrepreneurs know their own and their firm's limitations. They know there will times when they need to pull back the throttle rather than throwing caution to the wind by going full speed ahead. It is at those times that it takes courage to say "Whoa!" rather than "Let's go!"

Real Entrepreneurs Embrace and Foster Innovation

Firms succeed only to the extent they are better than the other firms in their market space. Innovation enables the firm to change the market space. Business strategists like Gary Hamel pose questions like, "What, if changed, would change everything?" and "What if it could be done would make your competitors irrelevant?" Innovation, if properly targeted, may have the potential to make your competitors' products and/or services obsolete.

Innovation applies to products, services and processes. It even applies to business models. The "degree of newness" also applies to innovation. The degree of newness can be classified as new to the firm, new to that market segment, new to the industry, and new to the world. An idea can be new or it can be the application of an existing idea in a new way. It can involve being the first business to install a drive-in window or to deliver the product to the customers. Innovation can involve being the first in your industry to use one or both of these approaches even though they may be common in another industry. Innovation can also involve using existing technology in an innovative way as Apple did when it persuaded Corning to make its Gorilla glass for its "i" products.

Savvy entrepreneurs recognize that fostering innovation involves: (1) never accepting the status quo, (2) continuously listening to the market for "pain points," (3) being willing to experiment, and (4) accepting the fact that most of your innovative ideas may not make it to market or succeed when they get there. Entrepreneurs therefore need to practice "smart innovation" by adopting "Stage-Gate®" like processes developed by Robert Cooper[6] that increase their odds.

Cautionary Note: The classic line from Field of Dreams "If you build it, he will come." is just a modern version of the "If you build a better mousetrap, the world will beat a path to your door." Many entrepreneurs get caught up in trying to make their products better by adding more and more "whistles and bells." There is a big difference between benefits and features. Benefits are aspects of a product that the market values and will pay for. Features are product additions that the marketplace does not value at all or enough to pay for. After all, who wants to pay $29.95 for a stainless steel mouse evaporator when the 29¢ traditional spring-loaded mousetrap meets their expectations? Entrepreneurs need to remember that innovation is cool only if it adds value and provides their firms with a competitive edge. This ties into the previous section as well. There is no point in developing an innovative mousetrap where there isn't a mouse problem.

Concluding Thoughts – Like Moths Driven to the Flame

It should be clear by this point in the book that there is a big difference between real entrepreneurs and people who start businesses – particularly life style businesses that are clones of other businesses. For real entrepreneurs, sensing opportunities and seizing them are irresistible. When they can harness and capitalize on the characteristics profiled in this chapter and apply them to opportunities then they can change the world.

Some people define luck as "when preparation meets opportunity." I disagree. Success is what happens when preparation meets opportunity." The confluence of preparation and opportunity represents a "perfect entrepreneurial storm." An anonymous entrepreneur noted years ago, "Entrepreneurship is about having a few years of your life like most want, so you can live the rest of your life like most can't."

This chapter has noted how real entrepreneurs are like moths driven to a flame. It is appropriate that it closes with *"the lesson of the moth"* by Don Marquis.

the lesson of the moth *

i was talking to a moth
the other evening
he was trying to break into
an electric bulb
and fry himself on the wires.

why do you fellows
pull this stunt I asked him
because it is the conventional
thing for moths or why
if that had been an uncovered
candle instead of an electric
light bulb you would
now be an unsightly cinder
have you no sense

plenty of it he answered
but at times we get tired
of using it
we get bored with the routine
and crave beauty
and excitement.
fire is beautiful
and we know that if we get
too close it will kill us
but what does that matter
it is better to be happy
for a moment
and be burned up with beauty
than to live a long time
and be bored all the while.
so we wad all our life up

into one little roll
and then we shoot the roll
that is what life is for.
it is better to be a part of beauty
for one instant and then cease to
exist than to exist forever
and never be a part of beauty
our attitude toward life
is come easy go easy
we are like human beings
used to be before they became
too civilized to enjoy themselves.

and before I could argue him
out of his philosophy
he went and immolated himself
on a patent cigar lighter
I do not agree with him
myself I would rather have
half the happiness and twice
the longevity

but at the same time I wish
there was something I wanted
as badly as he wanted to fry himself

archy

Chapter Two

THE ROLE OF MENTAL HEALTH IN ENTREPRENEURISM

"Life in a startup is similar to the cycle of manic-depressive behavior where you feel you are on the top of the world one day and waking up terrified in the middle of the night on the next."
Anonymous founder of a technology firm

Mental health is characterized as the presence of various emotional conditions that affect one's behavior that, in turn, may produce favorable consequences. People are considered to be mentally healthy if they have a sense of reality, a sense of perspective, a sense of patience, and a sense of humor, as well as the ability to handle setbacks in a constructive manner. The concept of *balance* plays a key role in one's mental health. Balance applies to the ability to balance one's work with one's personal life. Balance also applies to the ability to balance long-term and short term issues. It also applies to living one's life according to one's priorities and living a life with minimal regrets.

Mental disorders can be described as the lack of balance. The lack of balance may occur under various conditions including:

- When people are so fixated on something that they are not able to function in a constructive manner.
- When situations call for flexibility but people cannot adapt.
- When reality calls for new learning and people will not change their attitudes and/or behavior.
- When people are obsessed with something to the point that they are delusional.

- When people are so compulsive or addicted that they cannot help themselves.
- When people choose to deny reality.
- When people rationalize reality to suit themselves rather than confront it.
- When people fail to accept responsibility for situations and use scapegoats so they do not have to blame themselves when things go awry.

In summary, something is considered a mental disorder if it: (1) dominates one's approach to life, (2) has detrimental effects, and (3) the person is unwilling or unable to change what one thinks and does.

This chapter profiles how various dimensions of an entrepreneur's personality can contribute to an entrepreneur's success or failure. The basic premise of this book is that it is the lack of being normal that sets successful entrepreneurs apart and contributes to their ability to sense and seize opportunities. The last chapter included numerous cautionary notes. They indicated how, like most things on life, having certain qualities can be advantageous. Yet they also indicated that almost anything in excess or taken to an extreme can have detrimental consequences. This chapter takes a closer look at the consequences that can be attributed to entrepreneurs whose behavior can be considered to not be normal and even to the point of being the product of mental disorders.

In the 1960s IBM was in its *first* prime. Thomas Watson Jr. as CEO encouraged his people to "Think." He wanted his people to spend more time thinking rather than all their time "doing." When Steve Jobs returned to Apple, he encouraged Apple's people to "Think Different." He assumed that if they thought different, they would "do different" and by doing different Apple could reestablish its greatness.

This chapter focuses on how entrepreneurs think and act differently – and to what extent doing so may be beneficial or harmful. It may be helpful to recognize there are different levels of "thinking different" and "doing different." Some ways of thinking and behaving are considered normal. Yet what is considered *normal* is usually defined by *normal* people. Behavioral scientists have noted for decades that what is normal in one society or culture may be considered far from normal in another society or culture. This chapter will address normalcy from a U.S. perspective. I have also taken the liberty (a writer's prerogative or license) of simplifying a lot of the thinking about mental health and disorders to benefit the reader and to keep this book from being as long as *War and Peace*.

The Normal to Insanity Continuum

It would be too simplistic to say a person is either normal or not normal. It may be helpful to approach this chapter by indicating there is a continuum with normalcy at one end and insanity at the other end. Figure 1 profiles the Normal to Insanity Continuum.

Figure 1

The Normal to Insanity Continuum

Normal ------ Weird ----- Crazy ----- Insane

It should be noted that each dimension on the continuum has considerable band width. Some people are so normal that they are predictable and boring. Other people may be considered rather normal even though they may approach certain things differently than other normal people. For example, some people put both socks on before they put on their shoes. Other people put a sock and shoe on one foot at a time. While they may approach the task differently, both groups would be considered normal people - just as people who are left handed are considered to be fairly normal by right handed people.

Scott Adams' *Dilbert* comic strip may help clarify normalcy. Like Dilbert, we all do dumb things and some people are dumber than others! The nature and frequency of dumb things determines whether people are *normal* - who occasionally do dumb things or whether they are truly stupid by doing a lot of dumb things or the same dumb things again and again. The same applies to the *normalcy* of one's behavior.

Let's Take a Closer Look at Weirdness

Michael Lazerow provided an interesting perspective of the role weirdos can play in his article, "Why Weirdos Outperform Normals."[7] Here are some of the characteristics and noteworthy accomplishments of people who normal people consider to be weird:

- Weirdos see the world as a blank slate for them to paint their masterpiece. Forget marching to their own drums. They make up their own instruments. Forget thinking outside the box. They don't see boxes. They see circles and horizons and trapezoids.
- Weirdos don't see anything as impossible. Anything is possible. Just give us enough time.
- Weirdos are contrarians. They think differently and act even more differently. Normals try to fit in. Weirdos stick out without really trying.
- Weirdos aren't driven by money. Money is a destination. Weirdos are all about the journey.
- Weirdos don't care what others think. They only care THAT they think and want to change HOW they think.
- Weirdos come in all shapes and sizes, colors and countries. And they're not new to the tech industry, or industry in general.
- Weirdos thought it made sense to get on the Mayflower from England to settle in a new land.
- Weirdos thought we should get rid of slavery.
- Weirdos insisted that women should also have a vote.

Michael Lazerow offered the following observations and suggestions:

- The world would suck if it weren't for weirdos.
- Instead of trying to get our kids to fit in, we should help them celebrate why they are different.
- Let's start to teach kids to embrace weird. Weird is good.
- And let's not stop until weird is normal.

Tony Hsieh, who transformed Zappos into an incredible internet business, also believes being weird – in the right context and not to the extreme – can have numerous benefits. He noted, "One of the things that makes Zappos different from a lot of other companies is that we value being fun and being a little weird...This means that things we might do might be a little unconventional – or else it wouldn't be weird. We're not looking for crazy or extreme weirdness though. We want just a touch of weirdness to make life more interesting and fun for everyone...One of the side effects of encouraging weirdness is that it encourages people to think outside the box and be more innovative."[8]

Entrepreneurs, like other people, have personal idiosyncrasies. And like non-entrepreneurs, their idiosyncrasies can be so pronounced and/or frequent that they can have detrimental effects. When a person's idiosyncrasies are excessive and produce unfavorable consequences, then they may be considered mental disorders. In extreme cases, certain behaviors may be considered one or more forms of mental illness. An entrepreneur's idiosyncrasies may even evolve to become neurotic or even psychotic behavior.

When a person's thought patterns and/or behavior are what statisticians consider to be "one standard deviation from the mean," then that degree of being different may be considered a bit weird by normal people. One standard deviation from the mean usually covers about two-thirds of the population's behavior. Being one standard deviation from the mean puts a person on the outer edge of two-thirds of the population.

A beer drinking example may illustrate the degrees of difference. Two-thirds of beer drinkers would include people who drink most brands of beer as well as light and dark beers. A person who drinks beer with ice in it, however, may not be in the two-thirds. They may be considered weird by most normal beer drinkers. To illustrate the band width of weird, consider how that person would be perceived by normal beer drinkers if that person has ice in his/her beer and blends it with lemonade, iced-tea, or even tomato juice. Normal people would consider such behavior to be extremely weird - and possible borderline crazy!

It is safe to say that the "blended" beer preference would be at least two standard deviations from the mean. Few people would even conceive of those blends – let alone drink them. Ironically, in extremely hot climates like Phoenix, such combinations are not that extreme. The ice makes the beer more refreshing. The lemonade or iced tea thins the beer so it goes down easier. Blending tomato juice with beer raises eyebrows for even some of the more venturesome Phoenicians. Instead of wincing, try the ice and blends some time - I lived in Arizona for over six years. I was considered quite weird - possibly three standard deviations from the mean - because I did all the concoctions including the ice with non-alcoholic beer!

Two standard deviations encompass 95.4 percent of a population's behavior. This means about one person in twenty demonstrates markedly different behavior. To be three standard deviations from the mean, however, is quite different. It encompasses 99.7 percent of the behavior exhibited by people. In simpler terms, it means that one in 333 people exhibit a certain type or range of behavior. Being two standard deviations from the mean may be an indication that a person is a bit weird. If the behavior has negative consequences, then it could be neurotic behavior. Some people may even consider such behavior to be a form of mental illness. Being three standard deviations from the mean may make the person seem a bit crazy – or even psychotic. Insanity, fortunately, tends to be more than three standard deviations from the mean.

Entrepreneurs Create and Connect the Dots

The degree of difference in one's thinking and behavior raises the point made throughout this book. Even though the continuum seems to identify behaviors that are different from normal behavior, the differences can, in fact, be beneficial. After all, innovation comes from thinking and doing differently. Steve Jobs' *Think Different* ad notes that while some people are seen as crazy, they may in fact be geniuses. He noted that people have to be crazy to think they can change the world – and yet some of them do.

While I would not consider Steve Jobs to be a role model, his different approaches produced a plethora of products that changed the way we live and work. Steve Jobs had many talents. One of the talents was the ability to connect the dots between seemingly unrelated things. When he dropped out of the standard classes at Reed College he dropped in on a calligraphy class. He credited that class as the inspiration for developing the fonts for the Macintosh – which changed desk top publishing forever.

One of the benefits of having a liberal arts education is that it exposes students to a wide variety of ideas and perspectives. The ideas and perspectives have the potential to be the "dots" that connected later in life have the potential to foster mental breakthroughs and innovation. Travel can provide a person with a variety of experiences that can be "dots." Interacting with a variety of people can also create "dots" that may lead to the cross-pollination of ideas that, in turn, leads to innovative ideas. One's intuitive skills also benefit from varied experiences. Training in non-linear thinking can also help foster innovative breakthroughs. When all of these factors come together, a person will look at the world differently, think different thoughts, and come up with different ideas.

The ability to see the world differently - to see things others don't see and to think thoughts others don't think - is one of the pillars for entrepreneurship. I cannot resist bringing up the film *The Sixth Sense* at this point in the book. One of the most memorable lines from the movie is spoken by the young boy who says, "I see dead people." That eerie line captures how many entrepreneurs see the world. Instead of dead people, they see opportunities that other people don't see.

Having a keen sense of reality and the ability to change reality are two of the qualities of great leaders. Another of Steve Jobs' talents that made him "different" was his propensity to operate in a "reality distortion field." He would mentally bend reality to fit his needs. He redefined situations to make things happen that would not otherwise happen. He had a never-ending propensity to challenge key assumptions and conventional wisdom. His contempt for the status quo led him to encourage his people to seek breakthrough innovations and to never settle for anything less than perfection – without regard to the cost in dollars and mental anguish for his people.

Steve Jobs never seemed to be tethered to the ways things have been done, the conventional, and linear thinking. His intuitive skills and the ability to look at situations from different perspectives enabled him to make mental leaps. The leaps and mental breakthroughs served as the basis for numerous innovations at Apple. His charisma and ability to get other people to think differently enabled his people at Apple to make the impossible possible and to make what he called "insanely great products."

Steve Jobs' greatest achievement may have been his ability to create an organization that was able to transform crazy ideas into leading-edge products, processes, and business models. These, in turn, contributed to Apple becoming the highest valued firm in the United States.

The Free American Dictionary defines genius as "a person with exceptional ability, especially of a highly original kind." Steve Jobs was considered by many people to have been a genius. According to the "Stanford-Binet" IQ score system, a genius is anyone with a 140 or higher IQ. People with a 140 IQ or higher make up only 2.2% of the population. I am not sure he ever had his IQ measured, but it is clear that Steve Jobs approached life with a very different mental framework. If being a genius involves having the ability to think thoughts that normal people cannot or do not think, then he was truly a genius.

Yet being a genius does not mean you are a genius at everything. One may be a genius in certain areas or fields and be rather aloof in other areas or fields. Mozart was an example of being a genius in certain areas but not others. He was gifted when it came to creating great music, but he may not have been a genius in developing interpersonal relationships and fitting in.

Fortunately, entrepreneurs do not have to be geniuses to be successful. Less-than-genius entrepreneurs have been able to create breakthrough products and processes. Having a great mind may help, but the ability to act on great thoughts is what separates the great firms from the pack. Jeff Bezos noted, "I think ideas are easy. It's the execution that's hard."[9]

A Closer Look at the Difference of Being a Visionary or Being Delusional

Some of the most successful entrepreneurs have been heralded as visionaries. Some of their success has been attributed to their ability to see what the future would or could hold and/or their ability to alter the future through their innovations and actions. Yet, having a vision can be a "Catch 22." It can be beneficial if your vision can be turned into a reality. Conversely, if one's vision does not become a reality, one may be considered by others to be a fool.

What is the difference between being a visionary and being delusional? Christopher Columbus had a vision for a new trade route to India. While he may not have found it, pursuing his vision lead him to explore uncharted waters. Ironically, Columbus has been described as an entrepreneur. Queen Isabella of Spain acted as a venture capitalist by sponsoring his voyage of discovery. Columbus' voyage also helped dispel the centuries old belief that the world was flat.

More recent examples of entrepreneurs who had visions for what could be and should be include Walt Disney, Fred Smith, Michael Dell, and Richard Branson. Walt Disney believed he could make a feature-length animated film. Many people in the industry called it Disney's Folly until he proved them wrong when it became one of the highest grossing films of all time. Young Michael Dell didn't know he was starting a major computer brand and company when he was a freshman at The University of Texas. It did not take much time for his innovative "Dell Direct" business model to challenge IBM.

Fred Smith created what is now known as FedEx when he envisioned a business that could deliver parcels almost anywhere in the world. Richard Branson's vision for a better way of doing many businesses prompted him to challenge established firms – including British Airways. When you take on a business supported by your own government, you have to believe in your vision and yourself. All four of these entrepreneurs envisioned what could be … what should be. They then made their visions a reality and changed the world.

If one's vision is extremely compelling, then it can provide the motivation to pursue it in spite of the odds or what other people, particularly normal people, think. Transforming one's vision into reality and proving the naysayers, skeptics, and cynics they were wrong can be redeeming and very rewarding. Conversely, one's vision can be such a fixation that it leads to obsessive/compulsive behavior. In this situation, the person may be more than a fool; he/she may be downright crazy.

It is one thing to have faith in one's vision or idea. It is another to pursue it well after the evidence is clear that it is delusional. It often takes having blind faith to pursue one's vision. Yet to be blind to the reality that it is not going to be fulfilled is when one's vision becomes what could be a lasting delusion. Psychiatrists define delusional as, "A belief that is so strongly held that it continues to be held in spite of invalidating evidence. If strong enough, it can be a symptom of mental illness." *The Encyclopedia of Mental Disorders* states, "Delusions are irrational beliefs, held with a high level of conviction, that are highly resistant to change even when the delusional person is exposed to forms of proof that contradict the belief."

Some people have defined success as what happens when you transform your dreams into reality. There is a point, however, where the vision may become a hallucination or even a schizophrenic condition. The term "Quixotic" comes from the book *Don Quixote* by Miguel de Cervantes. It notes that some people follow dreams that may be impossible, idealistic, or foolish. The lead character is a dreamer who tries to slay windmills thinking they are giants. His never-ending quest, in spite of the odds, makes him seem foolish in spite of his good intentions.

Many entrepreneurs are driven by their dreams. Some are able to fulfill them; some are not. The difference between the two groups may be whether their visions are possible and whether they are able to do what needs to be done to make them a reality. Thomas Edison noted, "Vision without execution is hallucination."

While normal people may consider something to be impossible or unlikely, real entrepreneurs see them as possible, likely, or even inevitable. Maurice Maeterlinck, a Nobel Laureate, noted the importance of having courage to move forward with their dreams - especially when confronted by naysayers. He stated, "At every crossway on the road that leads to the future each progressive spirit is opposed by a thousand men appointed to guard the past."

Peter Drucker echoed Maurice Maeterlinck's sentiment about visionaries who have the courage of their convictions. He noted in *Adventures of a Bystander,* "Whenever anything is being accomplished, it is being done, I have learned, by a monomaniac with a mission."

Steve Jobs' push for the development of the iPad illustrates the power of conviction and how entrepreneurs often have to make intuitive leaps. I remember the day the iPad was launched. The "talking heads" on one financial network noted they did not see any real value in such a product. They exclaimed, "Who would need this?" Because of my age I recognized the value right away – the larger screen made it is easier to read than a cell phone.

Steve Jobs envisioned what the iPad could do. It became one of the most successful product launches ever. Ironically, he led Apple to create products that became addictions – products even the "talking heads" could not imagine what life would be like without them. The iPad and other innovative products are examples of how entrepreneurs can be driven to introduce products that change the world. The difference between having a bold vision and pursuing folly is discussed more in the next chapter.

Patience May Be a Virtue, But it Can Be Elusive for Entrepreneurs that are Driven

Entrepreneurs who are driven to seize opportunities frequently are short on patience. Their lack of patience is understandable especially if they: (1) want to be the first mover, (2) believe competition may be quick to respond, and (3) sense the window of opportunity may have a limited duration.

This creates a sense of urgency for them which can be counterproductive. Their restlessness may keep them from getting key information, from testing their assumptions, and from getting the timing right. It may cause entrepreneurs to "fire," when they need to take a moment to "aim." Their lack of patience may also hurt their relationships with their people and others. This is particularly true for people who work for them who do not exhibit their level of commitment.

There can be a fine line between moving too quickly and moving too slow. Entrepreneurial success is a function of knowing *what* needs to be done, knowing *how* to do what needs to be done, and knowing *when* to do what needs to be done. As noted earlier in the book, Steve Jobs was known for exclaiming, "You have to drive a stake in the ground." when his people were caught up in discussions. He stressed focus and decisiveness. As noted earlier, the best entrepreneurs have the courage to step into the darkness. They have the courage to make decisions and to implement them in the absence of complete and timely information.

Yet entrepreneurs are not necessarily the first people to identify situations where people's needs are not being met and/or to develop a solution. They are, however, usually the first people to seize the moment by launching a product or service to address the need(s).

Andrew Weinreich, a social media entrepreneur noted, "Entrepreneurs are not the ones with the best ideas. They're just the ones willing to jump off a cliff without the answer." Ironically, after they seize the moment and/or offer an innovative solution, people - including their competitors often exclaim painfully, "Why didn't we see that, think of it, and/or develop it?"

Entrepreneurs Need to Focus, but They also Need to Have Multiple Perspectives

Steve Jobs' ability to connect disparate dots enabled him to have the mental breakthroughs that led to the development of innovative products. Sensing and seizing opportunities requires perceptiveness – the ability to see things others don't see. Sometimes this involves the ability to envision what can be or will be. Sometimes it involves merely being in a position to see something that others don't see because the others' perspectives may be too myopic.

Simply stated, you will only see what is in your perceptual field and you will only think thoughts that are in your mental field. Ironically, the problem or solution may be hiding in plain sight to those who are actively looking and who have a broader perspective.

Conventional thinking is like a set of blinders. The best entrepreneurs make a deliberate effort to adopt a 360 degree (also known as a kaleidoscopic) perspective. They recognize that like turning the chamber of a kaleidoscope, when they approach a situation from various vantage points they are likely to see things they did not see before turning the chamber. In many cases, the opportunity and/or solution may be so visible or apparent to them that they can relate to the phrase, "It was a blinding flash of the obvious." People who lack a kaleidoscopic perspective don't see the flash.

Lateral thinking is similar to having a kaleidoscopic perspective. Lateral thinking helps entrepreneurs discover opportunities and to develop or find solutions. It also helps entrepreneurs apply something that already exists to different and/or new market spaces. Lateral thinking helps entrepreneurs develop new solutions to existing problems. It also helps entrepreneurs find other users and uses for existing technology, products, and services.

Anticipatory thinking – like Wayne Gretzky's approach to playing hockey - helps entrepreneurs identify emerging opportunities. It also helps entrepreneurs develop solutions to problems that are not considered problems - yet. In this case, entrepreneurs who anticipate what the future may hold by asking "What if?" questions have a mental head start over their competitors. This gives anticipatory entrepreneurs time to develop innovative solutions. People who lack anticipatory thinking don't see the obvious and inevitable. Yet, as already noted, visionary entrepreneurs need to recognize the risk of being seen as crazy if they are too far ahead of their time.

Entrepreneurs Must be Innovative, but Using a Portfolio Approach is Best

A business succeeds only to the extent it has competitive advantages. As stated earlier, you have to be better than your competitors and to be better you have to be different. Being different, however, does not assure success. If your firm isn't better than its competitors on the things your target market values, then your firm is in jeopardy.

Being better usually involves being innovative. You have to develop things that set your firm apart and provide customers with a compelling reason to do business with your firm rather than your competitors. As noted earlier, Peter Drucker considered real entrepreneurs to be the ones who bring something new to the market place. He noted that if all you do is match what is already in the market, then you are not a real entrepreneur.

Innovation and weirdness have similarities. There is a degree of newness continuum. Figure 2 profiles the Innovation Continuum. Innovation can range from tweaking what the firm or one's competitors offer all the way to developing breakthroughs that make things possible that were not possible.

Figure 2

The Innovation Continuum

Minor modifications - Continuous improvement - Innovation - Breakthrough Innovation

Most successful firms have a balanced innovation portfolio. Some of their efforts are designed to continuously improve what they are doing while also developing innovative products and processes. While the "total quality movement" that started over thirty years ago continues to emphasize the need for continuous improvement, Tom Peters observed that if you're 100% into continuous improvement, you'll doubtless give breakthrough innovation short shrift.[10]

Innovation can also be framed in the context of the "degree of newness." Figure 3 profiles the Degree of Newness Continuum. The degree of newness continuum profiles the breadth of impact of the innovation.

Figure 3

Degree of Newness Continuum

New to the firm - New to the market - New to the industry - New to the world

Continuous improvement is more in the "new to the firm" category. Innovation may involve internal processes, but it tends to be targeted to the market. New to the world innovation is similar to the impact of breakthrough innovation. Being new to the firm is like changing your address. Being new to the world is like changing the way the world lives and/or works.

Innovation is also tied to exploration. The firm is innovative if it pursues opportunities or markets it has not served. Figure 4 profiles the Degree of Exploration continuum.

Figure 4

Degree of Exploration Continuum.

Different market segments - Different markets - New markets - New industries

Exploration has its merits if it is approached properly. The least risky approach involves exploring market segments that are somewhat different from what the firm is currently serving but still enables the firm to leverage its current capabilities, products, and services. The targeted customers may be different, but the firm may not have to make major changes or to be highly innovative. Most of the changes may involve tailoring the firm's offerings to one or more different target market(s). In most cases, the firm is not exiting its current market. This enables the firm to fund its exploration from its current resources.

When the firm explores different markets rather than an adjacent segment in its current market space, it usually involves making more significant changes. It may also require innovation. The firm may need to develop new products and processes. This strategy usually requires more lead time, more resources, and different capabilities.

When the firm explores new markets – possibly markets in a different industry, then the firm will almost certainly have to be more innovative. It will need to develop all new products, all new processes, and all new capabilities. To say this degree of exploration is a stretch would be an understatement. To do so also tends to involve considerable risk. Any time a firm goes where it has not gone before and tries to do what it has not done before, it involves risk. Some firms try to reduce the risk by imitating what the other firms in that market space may be doing. Imitation may be easier than innovation, but it does not provide any competitive advantages.

The greatest degree of exploration involves exploring virgin market space. Virgin market space involves exploring a new market space in an industry that is just beginning. To modify the *Star Trek* phrase, it involves "Boldly going where no or few firms have gone." New industries usually require new business models – which require considerable innovation. New business models usually require new capabilities and new skills. These also take time to develop.

Entrepreneurs who explore on this level do not have the benefit of a wealth of market information or the existence of best practices. This level requires a lot of innovation and experimentation. The entrepreneur will need to seek the best information available, but the firm will probably have to use a launch and learn strategy to find out what the nascent market wants and what works.

It should be apparent at this point that innovation and exploration often go hand in hand. These two business strategies can be plotted with the degree of innovation as the horizontal dimension and degree of exploration as the vertical dimension. Each dimension can then be scored from low to high. The Innovation and Exploration Matrix in Figure 5 profiles the various combinations of exploration and innovation.

Each cell calls for different capabilities, time horizon, and resources. Entrepreneurs who operate in Cell #1 are like caretakers. While it may not seem like they are not taking much risk, their lack of commitment to innovation will cause any competitive advantage they may have to erode and ultimately vanish. Their lack of exploration means their firms are in quicksand. Their declining market share in a single market segment will cause their demise.

Entrepreneurs who are in Cell #2 do not commit many resources to innovation. They may be committed to continuous improvement, but true innovation is not part of their growth strategy. Their growth strategy involves leveraging their current capabilities to capitalize on markets they have not served and/or targeting emerging markets. While their exploration should be commended, their success may be short-lived. First-movers often become the targets for other firms. First movers who are not committed to innovation rarely enjoy sustained competitive advantages.

Figure 5

Innovation and Exploration Matrix

	Low — Degree of Innovation — High	
High Degree of exploration	**Cell #2** — Applying current capabilities to different or new market space.	**Cell #4** — Path-making firm that develops innovative solutions for emerging problems/opportunities.
Low	**Cell #1** — Maintaining the status quo. Little chance for future success.	**Cell #3** — Developing competitive advantages in current or similar market space.

Degree of Innovation

Entrepreneurs who are in Cell #3 may combine continuous improvement and innovation in an effort to strengthen their competitive positions. This approach will be effective only as long as the firm is in markets that have solid futures. Firms that are better than their competitors in mature or declining markets have to work hard just to keep growing or going.

Entrepreneurs who are in Cell #4 are committed to continuous innovation and exploration. They recognize that what worked well yesterday will not work as well today, will be even less effective tomorrow, and obsolete soon after that. Their firms are ever-evolving enterprises.[11] Entrepreneurs in Cell #4 also recognize that unless their firms have a substantial influx of capital the only way to explore and innovate is to have a deliberate and sustained program for reducing and or eliminating some of the things their firms are currently doing.

Each of the cells in the matrix involves a different degree of risk. Each strategy is influenced by the entrepreneur's comfort zone. Entrepreneurs in Cell #1 avoid risk by not changing what their firms are doing. They do not recognize that as someone once noted, "The greatest risk is not to take a risk." Entrepreneurs in Cell #2 stay in their comfort zone by continuing to offer minor modifications of their firm's products, services, processes and technology to different sets of customers. These entrepreneurs will be even more comfortable if they keep their current customers as well – at least in the short to medium term.

Entrepreneurs in Cell #3 usually enjoy finding new ways to do things and new things to do for their current and/or similar types of customers. Their comfort zone comes from being customer-centric to a specific targeted customer or similar customer segments. As long as their firm's offerings are in sync with their targeted customers' ever-evolving expectations, they may do well.

Entrepreneurs in Cell #4 have markedly different comfort zones from the other entrepreneurs. They are comfortable doing what they have not done before. Their radar is constantly exploring the horizon for new opportunities. They are prepared to boldly go where no firm has gone before and to introduce first-generation products and services. Entrepreneurs in Cell #4 approach their worlds with two particular premises. First, they believe that just because something hasn't been done, doesn't mean it can't be done. Second, they believe that just because you haven't done it, doesn't mean you can't do it.

Entrepreneurs in Cell #4 are the drivers of what Joseph Schumpeter called "creative destruction." Schumpeter considered creative destruction to be essential for the health of an economy. Their firms are the innovators that shatter the status quo of the existing products and services. They don't think outside the box – because they don't even see the box! They are perpetual optimists. They know there has to be a better way – even if they have to create it. Entrepreneurs in Cell #4 change the world by ignoring the rules, breaking the rules, and changing the rules. They make their competitors' products obsolete. They make their competition irrelevant.

Before moving on to the next section it may be worthwhile to take a closer look at the nature of imagination and the degree of innovation. Imagination can be the lifeblood of innovation. Imagination involves thinking new thoughts. Often, it leads to developing breakthrough products, services, processes, and business models. Imagination can be closely tied to tapping one's intuitive processes. One's intuitive processes are not constrained by conventional (inside the box) and/or linear thinking.

Tom Peters noted that if you want to have major innovation, then you need to set very ambitious goals for innovation. He noted the best way to break away from conventional thinking and continuous improvement is to set "10X" goals. He believed that if you set the goal of being .10X or ten percent faster, higher quality, cheaper, or more convenient, then you may try to do it by tweaking what the firm is currently doing.[12]

If you set a 10X – or ten times faster, ten times more convenient, ten times the level of quality, or one-tenth the cost/price, then people will have to be truly innovative. By setting a 10X goal, you must break away from what is being done. The beauty of the 10X goal is that even if you do not achieve it, your firm will be far more innovative than if you set a .10X goal.

Cautionary Note: Entrepreneurs who have an extreme imagination may be so far removed from reality that their ideas are considered bizarre by the marketplace – at least at that time. Entrepreneurs with extreme imaginations are often considered to be more than a bit neurotic. If they see things (market opportunities) others don't see and think thoughts (products and services) that no one has ever thought, then normal people may consider them to be delusional or even psychotic.

An Entrepreneur's Mental Health is Tied Closely to How Setbacks are Handled

A serial entrepreneur and venture capitalist noted, "As an entrepreneur, you face unrelenting pressure." Someone else observed, "As an entrepreneur, you'll have a crisis every day and a disaster every week." The last chapter noted that real entrepreneurs relish challenges and are driven to find solutions. It also noted how Jim Collins differentiates his concept of fallure from failure.

The ability to handle the setbacks that are inevitable when you create and manage ventures is a sign of mental health. While some people may consider a person to be mentally healthy because they seem to have self-confidence and a good attitude about life, the real test of mental health is the ability bounce to back after a setback, to learn from it, and to approach the world differently and smarter with renewed vigor.

Entrepreneurship is not for the faint hearted – especially if you want to change the world by doing things you and possibly no one else has done. Entrepreneurs must have considerable resilience and perseverance. The following quotations capture various perspectives about the nature of failure.

Putting Failure into Perspective

"There is no failure except in no longer trying."
Elbert Hubbard

"I'm convinced that about half of what separates the successful entrepreneurs from non-successful ones is pure perseverance."
Steve Jobs

"The greatest barrier to success is the fear of failure."
Sven Goran Eriksson

"Failure is not getting knocked down; it's not getting up again."
Vince Lombardi

"There is no failure. Only feedback."
Robert Allen

"Only those who dare to fail greatly can achieve greatly."
Robert Francis Kennedy

"Success is not final. Failure is not fatal."
Winston Churchill

"Failure is success if we learn from it."
Malcolm Forbes

"I don't know the key to success, but the key to failure
is trying to please everybody."
Bill Cosby

"Failure is only the opportunity to begin again more intelligently."
Henry Ford

"You always pass failure on your way to success."
Mickey Rooney

"The number of times I succeed is in direct proportion to the
number of times I can fail and keep on trying."
Tom Hopkins

Dr. Jekyll or Mr. Hyde?

Every person has his or her own idiosyncrasies. For entrepreneurs, their idiosyncrasies may be what drive them to start ventures and contribute to their success. For the rest of the world, their idiosyncrasies may keep them from starting ventures.

Entrepreneurial success has often been attributed to thinking and operating "outside the box." The willingness of entrepreneurs to challenge the status quo and conventional wisdom often makes them appear irrational to normal people. Yet it should be recognized that to the people exhibiting the behavior, their behavior seems quite logical. It is only irrational to outsiders, including normal people and other entrepreneurs, who do not see the world through their eyes.

Being decisive, focused, committed, and/or irreverent can be beneficial to the entrepreneur and his or her venture. Yet if any of these qualities are taken to the extreme, then they can be liabilities rather than assets. The same applies to certain business practices. Tom Peters' and Robert Waterman's book, *In Search of Excellence,* has been one of the best-selling business books of all time. Their list of eight factors that contribute to excellence became the basis for various corporate crusades. Tom Peters and Robert Waterman did an excellent job profiling how many of the most successful firms at the time the book was written demonstrated a bias for action, the ability to stick to the knitting, being close to customers, and five other factors. While each of the characteristics may help serve as a guide in efforts to improve performance, they can backfire if they are taken to their extreme.

Having a bias for action can help managers slay the procrastination dragon and reduce the tendency to succumb to paralysis by analysis. If one's bias for action is unbridled, however, then it can be reckless. Being close to your customers can help increase your business's top line. Yet having a preoccupation with your current customers and their current needs can keep the firm from recognizing what customers may want in the future and what non-customers want that may be even more lucrative.

If all of your attention is directed to the present and things within your reach, then you are managing by Braille. Sticking to the knitting - focusing on what the firm does well and is currently doing - can keep a firm from exploring new areas and developing new competencies. Sticking to the knitting may help a firm focus its attention and resources, but it may keep the firm from seeing emerging opportunities. Someone once observed, "If you stay in one business long enough, you will go out of business."

Conclusion: Entrepreneurs Need to Be Crazy in Moderation

This book distinguishes between *constructive* craziness and *dysfunctional* craziness. It also profiles how craziness needs to be in moderation. If the business is a B to C business, then it succeeds to the extent that it improves people's lives. If it is a B to B business, then it succeeds to the extent it improves its customers' profits. A business is successful to the extent that it has competitive advantages.

A business's competitive advantages are almost always based on innovation. Innovation is frequently based on looking at the world differently, thinking differently, and acting differently. Entrepreneurs who demonstrate these qualities may seem crazy at first to *normal* people, but when they change the world, their craziness is welcomed and rewarded.

"The men who try to do something and fail are infinitely better than those who try to do nothing and succeed."
Lloyd Jones, New Zealand author

Chapter Three

A CLOSER LOOK AT MENTAL DISORDERS

*"Entrepreneurship is the last refuge for the trouble
making individual."*
Natalie Clifford Barney, American
Playwright and novelist

Each of the qualities profiled in Chapter One can be a *Catch 22*.
Entrepreneurs who lack one or more of the qualities profiled in that
chapter may keep them and/or their ventures from having a
competitive edge. Conversely, too much of one or more of the
qualities can have negative effects. It is time to take a closer look at a
number of entrepreneurial behaviors to see what could happen if they
are excessive. Chapter five takes an even closer look at certain
behaviors and mental disorders.

Some entrepreneurs are *dyslexic*. This may explain why they
view the world differently. Some entrepreneurs have *attention deficit
disorder*. This may explain why they have little tolerance for
organizational routine. Some entrepreneurs were raised by
overbearing parents. This may explain why they have contempt for
authority and an aversion to working for someone else. Some
entrepreneurs were misled or cheated earlier in their lives. This may
explain why they are a bit paranoid. Some entrepreneurs were told
they would not amount to anything. This may explain why they are
driven to *become somebody* and prove those people wrong. One
entrepreneur supposedly named his business SITBR to note that
Success Is The Best Revenge.

Some Thoughts about Weirdness, Craziness, Madness, and Insanity[13]

"THE EDGE, there is no honest way to explain it because the only people who really know are the ones who have gone over. The others, the living, are those who pushed their controls as far as they could handle it and then pulled back or slowed down."
Hunter S. Thompson, *The Edge*

"Crazy people are considered mad by the rest of the society only because their intelligence isn't understood."
Wei Hui

"We do not have to visit a madhouse to find disordered minds; our planet is the mental institution of the universe."
Johann von Goethe

"I've got about ten things to say to you right now. But at least nine of them would make me sound like a psycho."
Lisa Kleypas, *Smooth Talking Stranger*

"You have no idea how crazy I am. I should be wearing yellow Caution tape, I'm that bonkers."
Robin Benway, *The Extraordinary Secrets of April, May & June*

"What I've learnt - to my cost - on several occasions in my life, is that people will put up with all manner of bad behaviour so long as you're giving them what they want. They'll laugh and get into it and enjoy the anecdotes and the craziness and the mayhem as long as you're doing your job well, but the minute you're not, you're f----d (expletive edited). They'll wipe their hands of you without a second glance."
Russell Brand, *My Booky Wook*

"When the whole world is crazy, it doesn't pay to be sane."
Terry Goodkind, *The Pillars of Creation*

"The object of life is not to be on the side of the majority, but to escape finding oneself in the ranks of the insane."
Marcus Aurelius

"A person needs a little madness, or else they never dare cut the rope and be free."
Nikos Kazantzakis

"In a mad world, only the mad are sane."
Akiro Kurosawa

"Whenever you find yourself on the side of the majority, it's time to pause and reflect."
Mark Twain

"A time will come when the whole world will go mad. And to anyone who is not mad they will say: 'You are mad, for you are not like us.'"
Attributed to St. Anthony the Great

"Sometimes I think that the greatest sign that there is intelligent life somewhere in the universe is that it hasn't tried to contact us yet."
Bill Watterson, *Calvin and Hobbes*

"Of course I'm crazy, but that doesn't mean I'm wrong."
Robert Anton Wilson, Science Fiction writer

"It's okay to be crazy, but don't be insane."
Puff Daddy

"I don't want to think about how many people have thought or still think that I'm crazy."
Dean Kamen, inventor and Founder of DEKA Research & Development Corporation

"Those who danced were thought to be quite insane by those who could not hear the music."
This quote has been attributed to either Angela Monet or Anne-Louise-Germaine de Staël

"In order to act, you must be somewhat insane. A reasonably sensible man is satisfied with just thinking."
George Clemenceau, former Prime Minister of France

Bold Action: Brilliant Visionary or Arrogant Fool?

Visionary entrepreneurs are heralded for "boldly going where no one has gone." They accept risks that others will not accept. They leap into the darkness by offering innovative ideas, concepts, products, processes, and services.

Mark Twain observed, "The man with a new idea is a crank - until the idea succeeds." Confidence plays a critical role in entrepreneurism. When you operate at the entrepreneurial edge you need considerable confidence to operate without a road map or a net. Entrepreneurs must believe: (1) they have what it takes to make the thousands of decisions that have to be made, (2) there is truly a gap in the market, (3) they can provide a superior product or service, and (4) their venture will make enough money to make it worth all the risk.

Savvy entrepreneurs have the ability to size up the uniqueness of the situation. They are like emergency room physicians that are skilled at triage. They are able to identify the important and urgent issues and separate them from the superficial and less pressing issues. Their ability to collect and analyze the most salient information as well as their ability to identify, evaluate, and prioritize possible courses of action enable them to reduce risk by making quick and informed decisions.

Fred Smith and the late Steve Jobs have been considered by many people to be courageous visionaries. Yet they both noted that they did not consider their ventures to be very risky. They believed they were launching firms (Federal Express and Apple Computer) that would capitalize on *inevitable* opportunities. Steve Jobs recognized the shortcomings and frustrations associated with large mainframe computers so he worked with Steve Wozniak to develop a user-friendly personal computer. Fred Smith recognized the growing need for quick and dependable delivery of parts and parcels. In his mind, starting Federal Express was not a leap of faith, nor was it overly risky. He wanted to ride the overnight delivery wave as it was being formed.

Yet to boldly go where no one has gone can put an entrepreneur on a fast track to disaster. There comes a point where unbridled confidence becomes arrogance. Boldness can border on being a mental disorder if the entrepreneur either chooses to not seek or incorporate useful information that is readily available or operates with the attitude "I've already made up my mind; don't confuse me with the facts."

The difference between success and failure in many cases is a matter of timing. If you offer the market a product or service before the market is ready, then your firm's offering will be like a grape that dies on the vine without being picked. Conversely, if you have the ability to be the first mover but are overly cautious and wait until the market is clearly ready for your product or service offering, then you run the risk of watching a less cautious firm preempt your launch.

Entrepreneurs must operate at the edge, but they should not blindly throw themselves off it. There is a big difference between starting a venture to serve needs that are not being met and boldly going where no market exists or may never exist. Entrepreneurs who temper their desire to be bold with reasonable anticipation and preparation are often called visionaries. Entrepreneurs who do not temper their boldness with wisdom are considered fools.

Being driven can be damaging if it is not tempered with a sense of reality. If one's passion to start a business is unbridled, then it may become an obsession. Kenny Rogers' song *The Gambler* emphasized (paraphrased) the need to know when to hold 'em, when to fold 'em, when to walk away, and when to run. Sports coaches may preach, "never give up!", but there comes a time when the wisest thing an entrepreneur can do is throw in the towel and cut one's losses. Many entrepreneurs hold on to their magnificent obsessions with such a death grip that they go down with the ship. Entrepreneur and business consultant Jon Vincent noted, "Don't attempt to ride a dead horse in hopes that it will come alive again."[14]

Savvy entrepreneurs recognize that startups are experiments that sometimes fail. They recognize when they have reached the point where their ventures cannot be revived. They learn from the experience and move on. Obsessive entrepreneurs deny reality or try to redefine it in such a way that that they are not able to move on to do different things or to do things differently.

If the entrepreneur is pointed in the right direction and has a keen sense of timing, then being obsessive may be beneficial. If, however, the entrepreneur is unable or unwilling to create an environment where other people are truly involved in directing the venture, then the entrepreneur's drive will merely be an exercise in futility.

The founder of a software firm noted, "Be bold. Make sure you aren't running with self-imposed limitations. The trials and tribulations in the early phases of starting a business can cause you to question your skills, your product, and possibly your mission." Howard Schultz demonstrated the power of his vision for having Starbucks become the "third place" – the place where people want to spend their time when they are not at home or work. His commitment to making his vision a reality gave him the perseverance he needed when he was seeking funding for Starbucks. He continued to seek investors when he was turned down more than one-hundred times.

The Desire to be Your Own Boss: Free at Last versus Freedom to be a Control Freak?

The desire to be an entrepreneur is often associated with the desire to be the master of one's destiny. Most entrepreneurs laugh when they are asked, "What it is like being your own boss?" They know first-hand that you have numerous bosses when you are an entrepreneur. They note that your customers will tell you what they want you to do and if you don't provide them with what they want, when they want it, where they want it, and at price they consider fair, then they will fire you! They know your customers are actually your employer. You can make payroll only to the extent that you meet your customers' expectations.

Entrepreneurs recognize that even though their names may be at the top of the organizational charts, they have to deal with employees who may challenge their ideas and who expect the business to adjust to their interests, schedules, and idiosyncrasies.

An entrepreneur from Tampa who was attending one of my seminars captured the frustration that some entrepreneurs feel - but seldom say out loud - about the challenges of managing employees.

When I asked the people at the seminar to describe the "ideal" business, she stood up and exclaimed, "One without employees!"

The following comments by three entrepreneurs capture the kinds of frustrations that cause people to start their own businesses. The founder of a software firm started his business because, "I just can't work for anyone else." This entrepreneur may have had a real aversion to authority or believed he was smarter than anyone else. Either of these reasons could have a detrimental effect on a new venture. The founder of a construction firm noted, "If I have to live by a dumb decision, then at least I will be the one to make it." He may not have had the egocentric attitude of the preceding entrepreneur, but his comment may indicate a reluctance to delegate authority to others in the venture or to seek outside advice.

The founder of a software services firm stated, "You should be able to eat what you kill. I was tired of getting such a small piece of the money that I earned." Her attitude is shared by a lot of entrepreneurs. They got tired of the people at the top getting all the benefits without doing all the work. Entrepreneurs who start businesses for this reason may be challenged when faced with a role reversal with their own people. In many cases, the people they hire may feel they deserve the same perks because the venture is the result of their blood, sweat, and tears. Savvy entrepreneurs empathize with the people they hire and make every effort to ensure the rewards are equitable and commensurate with the corresponding contributions.

Entrepreneurs with an excessive need for control can be their worst enemies. If their need to make sure everything is done right is unbridled, then they may be control freaks. Their fixation on checking every employee's actions can have a debilitating effect on new ventures. They jeopardize their venture's future because they rarely have the time to think strategically.

Their preoccupation with making sure nothing falls through the cracks and no one makes mistakes causes them to micromanage everything. Being a control freak can have devastating consequences. Entrepreneurs who are control freaks are usually unable to attract and keep good people. To make matters worse, they rarely solicit their employees' ideas, delegate decision making authority, or develop a successor. Their preoccupation with control creates a toxic work environment. A venture succeeds to the extent its people are mentally engaged and their talents utilized. Instead of coming up with ways to improve the venture's performance, employees spend their time making sure they don't make mistakes. The best employees quickly begin looking for an employer who will value their talents and engage their brains. In many cases, frustrated employees quit their jobs and start their own ventures as competitors to their control freak former employers.

Entrepreneurs who are control freaks seek people for their management team who will do what they are told. They also have people on their board of directors who will rubber stamp their decisions. Control freaks rarely seek advice, do not take direction or constructive criticism well, and do want to have their performance reviewed by others. Their "It's my way or the highway" attitude may alienate bankers, angel investors, and venture capital firms if they seek outside funding. Angels and venture capital firms who want to take their investments to the next level evaluate entrepreneurs to determine the extent they are "coachable." Entrepreneurs with unbridled egos may jeopardize their firms by breaking contracts, breaching covenants, and blatantly choosing not to obey the law!

The venture's management team and board of directors are a reflection of the entrepreneur's desire to have a professionally managed business. If entrepreneurs are truly committed to having exceptional enterprises, then they must bring in professionals to supplement their skills as they form their management teams. They will also need to seek outside board members who are objective and candid.

Savvy entrepreneurs recognize that they will have to learn to cope with situations in which they have little control. Coping can be seen as recognizing you may have to lose some battles to win the war. One entrepreneur noted in a tongue-in-cheek manner that he became so frustrated with the inconsistencies in the building code and the arbitrariness and pettiness of various inspectors that he had homicidal thoughts. He admitted that he may have what is known as the "Tower Syndrome." The entrepreneur indicated that he too had thoughts of climbing the church tower near City Hall and picking off the inspectors and code enforcement officers as they left their offices. To be frustrated is natural; to be homicidal is not normal.

That entrepreneur noted that you would have to be crazy to start a business – especially if you know in advance what you are getting into. He observed, "Who in their right mind would put themselves in a situation where they would have to deal with contractors who never keep their commitments and government bureaucrats who have more power than brains?"

Ironically, this entrepreneur has become very successful because he has found ways to move forward in spite of what most people consider to be a relentless series of barriers. His perseverance, resourcefulness, and resilience have given him the ability to forge ahead when most *normal* people would have given up and surrendered to the forces that defy common sense.

Before moving on, it should be noted that there is a big difference between being a control freak and someone who is committed to excellence and pays attention to detail. Control freaks never achieve excellence because they create environments that are constraining. Real entrepreneurs encourage and reward experimentation and innovation.

There is also a difference between being a control freak and a perfectionist. Control freaks are usually that way because they do not want to be vulnerable and they do not trust others to do the job on their own. Being a control freak has another consequence. Control freaks rarely develop successors.

Perfectionists are driven by pride and the desire to not make mistakes. Savvy entrepreneurs know that perfection takes twice as much time as excellence. They also know that, in most cases, the market does not require excellence. They recognize that consumers, whose needs are not being well or at all, are fairly forgiving as long as what their firm offers is better than what is available from other firms. They also know you cannot be the first mover if you demand that everything be perfect before you launch a business or its corresponding products or services.

Most Entrepreneurs Don't Like to be Fenced in

Someone described a jogger as either someone who either relishes the challenge of jogging so they can get more from their lives, or someone who is running away from something like family responsibilities, financial woes, or boring jobs. The first type of jogger seeks the adrenalin rush and high. The second type of jogger seeks sanctuary from certain realities. Actually, that person noted there is a third type of jogger. They are the ones who are chasing something they will never catch like invisible animals or immortality.

Some entrepreneurs start businesses because they are driven to fill market opportunities. They see market gaps where customers are in search of a business. Other entrepreneurs are like the second set of joggers. They seem to be driven by their desire to get away from a constraining environment as an employee rather than to capitalize on a market opportunity.

Some entrepreneurs started their firms because they found their jobs to be confining and stifling. They felt like the caged tigers in zoos that pace back and forth looking for a way to break out. They wanted the freedom to *do their own thing*. They wanted to no longer operate in an "organizational box." As already noted, entrepreneurs are not their own bosses. They still have to operate within some box. It may be their box, but it is still a box formed by various stakeholders who have their own expectations.

Yet, entrepreneurs who are trying to escape the repetition and tedium associated with working for someone else are in for a rude awakening. Once you start a business you go from being an entrepreneur to being the venture's chief executive officer. You are responsible for everything that needs to be done. The amount of *stuff* that needs to be handled is incredible. Entrepreneurs with a *stuff aversion* find that starting and running a venture is like being in a bad marriage. Their desire to start a business is overtaken by their desire to get out of the business.

Entrepreneurs, who are averse to doing the almost endless stream of *stuff* that must be done, may spend more time plotting ways to get out of their ventures than helping them grow. Some entrepreneurs put their businesses up for sale when they realize that the entrepreneurial honeymoon is over. Other frustrated entrepreneurs actually subvert their ventures through neglect.

When the founder of a communications and market research business was asked why she started her own business she stated, "I was fed up when I realized that I knew what to do, but I couldn't convince my boss to do it. I felt like I was living at home, with my parents still telling me what to do. … I was just getting too old for that shit." Her statement can be interpreted in numerous ways. She may have been fed up with being "bossed around." Some of today's top firms were created when constrained employees got tired of hearing, "Your ideas just don't fit in with what the firm is doing." and "Your ideas can't be funded at this time."

Yet in many cases, the constrained person's ego may have been larger than market demand or organizational realities. Having an idea does not guarantee that it will be a success. In many cases, their boss may have actually been right. Their ideas may not have had sufficient merit to be implemented.

Having the freedom to do your own thing sounds good until the wheels start falling off the wagon. Some entrepreneurs, especially first time entrepreneurs, are very naïve. They are not savvy to the realities of the business world or they just do not have the maturity needed to manage their emotions.

As noted earlier, many entrepreneurs are so arrogant that they will not accept advice and cannot take constructive criticism. In both cases, the entrepreneur's shortcomings can spell disaster. People who are very innovative, but do not have what it takes to be an entrepreneur need to recognize they may be better off finding a supportive employer than starting their own ventures.

Entrepreneurism: The Opportunity to Stand Out in the Crowd

The need for achievement can be a driving force for some people. Starting a venture is an avenue for some people to gain recognition and personal affirmation. People who are very competitive may view entrepreneurship as a way to stand out in the crowd. Other people view it as a way to test their abilities. Starting a successful business is clearly a very tangible achievement.

The need for achievement and recognition are closely related to one's self-concept. People who are driven to succeed can be extremely compulsive. The need for achievement may be so strong that no victory or set of victories - regardless of the degree of difficulty - will satisfy them. These people tend to be thinking about the next challenge before they even complete the current challenge.

Some people have such a strong need for recognition that they feel they always have to prove something to the world. The drive to prove they are worthy is frequently rooted in the desire to prove they are successful to the people who cast doubt on their competence earlier in their lives.

People with a damaged self-concept may embark on the entrepreneurial journey to prove their competence. Some entrepreneurs are so driven to prove that the other people were wrong about them become obsessed with building a high profile corporate headquarters. Their *edifice complex* can be very costly in dollars and the entrepreneur's time. Almost all emerging ventures are undercapitalized. They are also undercapitalized from a talent perspective. Every moment spent by entrepreneurs building monuments to their success is a moment that could have been invested in enhancing their ventures.

Ventures succeed to the extent they meet various stakeholders' expectations. If most of the entrepreneur's efforts are directed to proving others wrong, then the entrepreneur will not be investing enough time and attention to ensuring the firm is offering beneficial products and services to customers and creating a rewarding environment for the venture's employees.

Can Being an Entrepreneur Change One's Personality?

It is clear that certain personality factors may contribute to a person's propensity to be an entrepreneur. Meg Cadoux Hirshberg, however, raised an interesting point in an article in *Inc.* magazine. Her article focused on whether being an entrepreneur can change one's personality. She noted how the spouse of an entrepreneur was concerned because her husband's character and temperament had changed for the worse since he had started his business. The wife stated she hated what the business was doing to him because her husband was no longer the man she married.

Meg Cadoux Hirshberg's article focused on various issues including whether starting and running a business actually changes one's personality or if the daily challenges and stress reveal the entrepreneurs' true selves. She noted being an entrepreneur frequently evokes profound psychic responses and that it takes extraordinary character and resilience to live through the elation and depression. She also noted elation and depression can follow each other so rapidly that it induces emotional whiplash. Many of the people she spoke with confessed that starting their businesses made them less tolerant, and more competitive, rigid, demanding, and critical. She concluded with the need for entrepreneurs to be aware of their behavior so they do not slide into a psychic abyss.[15]

Conclusion: Real Entrepreneurs are "Hard-Wired"

Is entrepreneurism such an integral part of their DNA that real entrepreneurs cannot change or even retire? Can they resist the temptation to start a business when they see the marketplace composed of complacent, arrogant, and mediocre firms? Are they driven like Richard Branson who chartered a plane and sold seats on it rather than wait for the airline to meet his travel needs when his flight was cancelled? It is clear that real entrepreneurs like Richard Branson and countless others who are not on the covers of magazines are not like *normal* people. They sense and seize opportunities that make a difference in how we work and live.

"Am I or are the others crazy?"

Albert Einstein

Chapter Four

SERIAL ENTREPRENEURS AND MULTIPRENEURS:
ONE STARTUP IS NOT ENOUGH

*"I wake up every morning with a headache from thinking about
so many business ideas and opportunities."*
Bob Rippy, Serial & multipreneur

Is entrepreneurism a never-ending quest? Most successful
entrepreneurs see problems in the marketplace that represent business
opportunities. Their opportunity antennae are always scanning for
opportunities. They see opportunities even when they are not looking
for them. They see products, processes, and services that can be
improved and/or created. They believe there is always a better way to
do things and better things to do. Their minds go into hyper drive
whenever they hear people say, "I wish there was a business that ..."

Real entrepreneurs cannot turn their entrepreneurial mindset
off. They live with a 24/7 entrepreneurial clock that cannot be turned
off. They are not like *normal* people who can leave their jobs behind
them at the end of the day. The entrepreneurial clock is ticking every
minute of the day. It ticks when they are eating or trying to get a good
night's sleep. The entrepreneurial clock cannot even be stopped when
they are on vacation because their subconscious keeps bringing up
opportunities and/or ideas that need to be addressed. The voice from
within is constantly telling them they cannot let the opportunities to
improve their business or other business opportunities pass them by.

This book began by noting that not all entrepreneurs are alike.
Many entrepreneurs create ventures and stay with them until they

retire. They are either so committed to their ventures that they do not think about starting another business or they are so busy with their ventures that they cannot pursue an appealing opportunity if they see one. Other entrepreneurs, however, may start multiple ventures before they retire or die – whichever comes first.

People who start ventures in a sequential manner are called serial entrepreneurs. Most serial entrepreneurs identify with the t-shirt that has the caption, "So many bars and so little time!" that is sold in Key West. Serial entrepreneurs' lives can be summarized as, "So many opportunities and so little time!" Their entrepreneurial mindset identifies opportunities and a voice from within screams, "Seize them." Yet even serial entrepreneurs can experience "the glass is half-full" phenomenon. An anonymous serial entrepreneur noted, "Every day you come up with dozens of ideas, but you only have time to do two. Before long you go crazy."

Their propensity to continually look for new business opportunities can be so strong that they actively plan to seize the next opportunity while they are still involved in their current ventures. While most entrepreneurs relish what they have accomplished and plan to accomplish in their business, serial entrepreneurs live in a world full of opportunities *yet to be seized* by starting their next businesses.

The last decade saw the rise of a new breed of "here today, gone tomorrow" entrepreneurs. They may even plan the exit from their ventures before they even start them. Their goal is to get their ventures up and running as quickly as possible and then take them through some type of liquidity event. The liquidity event provides the opportunity to take their money to start their next venture or spend the rest of their days enjoying the good life in St. Barts. I believe the here today, gone tomorrow entrepreneurs are different from real entrepreneurs because real entrepreneurs want to build exceptional enterprises.

Entrepreneurs who want to build exceptional enterprises consider their ventures to be ends, not means. They identify with their firm's people, products, and customers. Entrepreneurs who start ventures for a liquidity event/exit tend to be far more self-centered. When a larger company buys an emerging company the larger firm usually keeps the best people, the intellectual property, and most valuable customers and then fires, sells off, liquidates, or ignores the rest.

Some serial entrepreneurs think "one or two ventures ahead." They are planning their next ventures before they even start their first or subsequent ventures. Entrepreneurs who have the goal of creating the next Google or Facebook approach their ventures in different ways than entrepreneurs who start their ventures hoping they will be acquired by Google. Entrepreneurs use different metrics if they are driven to grow their ventures than if they plan to cash out.

Some serial entrepreneurs are able to focus on the venture they are managing while they are growing it. Well-grounded serial entrepreneurs usually exit their business for one of three reasons. In the first case, they reach a certain point when they realize they should step aside and let someone else to manage their ventures. They may start another venture if they find another opportunity that appeals to them.

In the second case, they find another opportunity to pursue and step aside to pursue it. Most serial entrepreneurs are not able to focus solely on their current ventures because they are constantly thinking about the ventures they need to create so they can capitalize on the opportunities they want to seize. While most entrepreneurs get stressed out about not having enough capital to start and run their ventures, most serial entrepreneurs consider time to be their scarcest resource. They know they do not have enough time in their lives to seize all the opportunities they find. Most entrepreneurs are proud of what they created when they retire. Most serial entrepreneurs are destined to think about and regret the opportunities they did not seize.

In the third case, some serial entrepreneurs start new ventures because they find their current ventures too constraining. Soon after starting the ventures that they created because they felt confined by their previous employers, they feel confined by the similar expectations and responsibilities. In some cases, they may hire a professional manager so they are free to explore the things - like sales and/or new product development – that they enjoy doing in their firms. In other cases, they may sell their ventures to free them of the shackles of their current firms or to get the funds needed to pursue another new opportunity.

There is another group of entrepreneurs who start multiple ventures. They are called multipreneurs, concurrent entrepreneurs, or parallel entrepreneurs. The term multipreneurs will be used in describing and analyzing this group of entrepreneurs. Multipreneurs do not operate in a sequential fashion. Instead of watching opportunities pass them by or waiting to cash out of their current ventures, they seize the opportunities while continuing their involvement in some manner with their existing ventures. Multipreneurs who start numerous ventures in a relatively short period of time are like one-person conglomerates or one-person holding companies. Deniz Ucgasaran, Paul Westhead, and Mike Wright call them "portfolio entrepreneurs."[16]

Multipreneurs have certain similarities with serial entrepreneurs. Some pursue opportunities in related fields. Some develop ventures that are built on a core technology that spawns numerous product/service/new venture opportunities. Others are more diversified. They may create ventures in entirely different areas.

Richard Branson may be the world's leading multipreneur. His Virgin empire includes more than 200 businesses. When asked why he started various businesses including an airline, a train system, a cellular phone company, and a record label, he responded that the firms in those businesses were not doing things the way they could and should be done, so he created businesses to do those things right.

Being a multipreneur can be a challenging juggling act. Multipreneurs must have considerable mental dexterity and managerial acumen to direct multiple ventures. They also need to have a keen sense of timing. To modify the Kenny Rogers' lyric, they need to know when to start them, grow them, and when to part with them. Conventional entrepreneurs usually do not spend a lot of time thinking about when they will sell their businesses. Many entrepreneurs become serial entrepreneurs only after they sell their businesses. Rather than retire or work for someone else, they start subsequent businesses to seize another market opportunity. Most multipreneurs are different from serial entrepreneurs because they may actively seek additional opportunities while directing their ventures.

Few people have the mental dexterity needed to identify numerous opportunities and to start and manage numerous ventures in a sequential manner as serial entrepreneurs. Fewer people have the mental dexterity and managerial acumen to do it concurrently as multipreneurs. One of my elementary school science teachers noted that no one is able to juggle more than six objects at one time. He noted that trying to juggle more than six objects could drive you crazy. The teacher's premise may not have been right, but to try to juggle so many businesses that it jeopardizes one's health may indicate irrational and/or even masochistic tendencies.

Most conventional entrepreneurs are married to the businesses they create. While they may occasionally think about other business opportunities, they stay committed to their ventures until they retire or die. They may be tempted to start another venture to capitalize on a particular opportunity but they stay where they are because they do not want to spread themselves too thin or leave their comfort zone.

Most serial entrepreneurs don't marry their businesses; they date them. When they get them up and running they feel free to pursue another startup. Multipreneurs are more like people who "get or fool around." They prefer to date numerous businesses at one time.

Serial entrepreneurs and multipreneurs live by George Bernard Shaw's statement (often used by John and Robert Kennedy) from *Back to Methuselah,* "You see things as they are and ask, "Why?" I dream things as they never were and ask, "Why not?" They believe the best is yet to come. They find the process of starting ventures to be so mentally and/or financially rewarding that they keep "opportunity lists." One entrepreneur called his opportunity list his "Ventures to create before I die" list. Richard Branson not only keeps an opportunity list, he also encourages his employees to identify and suggest new venture opportunities.

Some serial entrepreneurs and multipreneurs find opportunities as a result of a deliberate and systematic search. Some are in a sense *drafted* into starting new ventures by customers, suppliers, or distributors that want them to provide certain products and services. When you do a great job in one business, your customers or other individuals and/or businesses may ask you to do other things to solve their problems including their outsourcing needs. Instead of creating a division to fill that need, multipreneurs create new ventures to provide those products or services.

Two examples demonstrate how a successful entrepreneur may become a multipreneur. In the first case, the founder of a packaging business was asked to develop a newsletter and handle corporate communications for one of his customers. The customer was so impressed with the entrepreneur's newsletter and internal communications that the customer volunteered to be the entrepreneur's first customer if the entrepreneur would start a business to meet that firm's needs.

In the second case, an entrepreneur did such a good job supplying parts for one of its customers, the customer encouraged the entrepreneur to set up a business that would assemble and inventory the customer's products. For these multipreneurs, the prospect of starting a business with at least one guaranteed customer made becoming a multipreneur an almost risk-free proposition.

Serial Entrepreneurs and Multipreneurs: How Do They Handle Success and Failure?

Not all serial entrepreneurs and multipreneurs have a perfect batting average. Some of their ventures may be failures. Looking at serial entrepreneurship from a decision tree perspective provides additional insight into what makes them tick and the differences even among serial entrepreneurs. Again, if the first venture is a success and the entrepreneur decides to make a career out of that venture, then that person is not a serial entrepreneur.

Some entrepreneurs do not create subsequent ventures even if their first venture is a success. Some even sell their ventures and return to regular jobs after a short period of time when they realize that entrepreneurial life does not meet their expectations, abilities, or life style. They are part of the "Been there, done it, got it out of my system" group of entrepreneurs. Psychologist Abraham Maslow asserted that a satisfied need no longer motivates behavior to satisfy that need. For others, however, the need to continue being an entrepreneur by starting one or more additional ventures remains alive.

If the first venture is a success and the entrepreneur either sells it or hires a professional manager to oversee its operations, then the entrepreneur is free to pursue the next venture. A number of things happen if the first venture is a success. Let's start with the good news. The entrepreneur is now a veteran entrepreneur. The entrepreneur has gained valuable experience, probably accumulated some capital, and developed a network of contacts he or she did not have when starting the first venture. Success in starting the first venture will also make it less difficult to secure debt and/or equity funding if needed. All of these factors should enable the entrepreneur to start the second venture more quickly. These factors should also increase the odds that the next venture will be successful.

Now let's look at the bad news. Some entrepreneurs succumb to the "Midas Touch" syndrome. They believe that because their first venture was a success they will be successful in starting almost any kind of business. This can have detrimental consequences. They may (1) not be as diligent in planning their next venture, (2) set overly ambitious goals, (3) take excessive risks, or (4) stray too far from their knowledge/skill/competency base. Any of these factors could contribute to the demise of their next venture.

The success of one's first venture may have another detrimental effect. Some entrepreneurs may not see their first venture as a verification of their entrepreneurial ability. They feel they need to start another venture to show that their first venture was the result of their talent rather than luck. They want to show that the entrepreneurial perceptiveness and skill that contributed to their first venture being in the right place at the right time with the right products was not an anomaly. Some people believe this is one of the reasons Steve Jobs was so driven to make NeXT succeed after he was forced to step down by the board of directors at Apple Computer. Starting a venture to prove something to one's self or others is not a good reason to start a business. If that is the only reason for starting a second venture, then serial entrepreneurship may be a mental disorder.

If the first venture fails and the entrepreneur recognizes that he is not cut out to be an entrepreneur, then that may be a reasonable and healthy way of handling the situation. That person usually does not become a serial entrepreneur at least at that point in his/her life. If the entrepreneur blames external forces such as predatory competition, a sagging economy, and so forth for their venture's failure, then the corresponding denial, rationalization, or use of other scapegoat defense mechanisms may indicate a mental disorder.

Yet the real issue is what drives the entrepreneurs who start a second venture after their first one fails. If the entrepreneur does an objective analysis of how he/she started and managed the first venture, then that is a good beginning. If the entrepreneur accepts responsibility for the lack of success, then that is a healthy sign. If the entrepreneur applies the "rule of finger" and reflects on how he could or should have done things better, then that is the beginning of the learning process that may contribute to a more successful second launch.

Someone once noted, "It's not what you know that kills you, it's what you don't know that kills you." To know what you don't know and to do something about it by learning new skills, by gaining additional experience working with someone else before starting the next venture, and/or by surrounding yourself with people who supplement your skills are healthy ways of dealing with the failure of the first venture.

Wilson Harrell who was an entrepreneur and publisher of *Inc. Magazine* referred to the entrepreneurial experience as "club terror." He considered certain aspects of being an entrepreneur to be as frightening as what he experienced as a downed airman behind enemy lines in World War II. He said club terror "is a private world filled with monsters sucking at every morsel of your being … [where] there can be no sleep … just wide-awake nightmares."[17]

Barry Moltz, author of *You Need to be a Little Crazy: The Truth About Starting and Growing a Business*, shares Wilson Harrell's view about entrepreneurship. He considers entrepreneurship to be a "Holy shit I could go bankrupt" situation. Yet it is interesting to note that even with the pain associated with having a business fail some entrepreneurs put themselves in a situation where they could fail again…and possibly again after that.

Unfortunately, some entrepreneurs fall prey to the "porcupine syndrome." Veterinarians note that many dogs that have had painful encounters with a porcupine exhibit an unusual response. Instead of learning to avoid porcupines, they seek them out for revenge. People who start a subsequent business to show others they are not failures violate the hot stove rule. They have not learned to avoid the hot stove.

Their fixation keeps them from learning and adjusting their mindset and behavior. When this is combined with their drive to show everyone was wrong in considering them to be a failure, their mindset and resulting behavior can be very dysfunctional. Albert Einstein captured the situation exhibited by entrepreneurs who do not learn from their experiences. He described insanity as "Doing something the same way but expecting different results."

If we follow the decision tree format, then the next set of branches looks at whether the serial entrepreneur's second venture was successful. If the first venture was successful and the second venture is successful, then the serial entrepreneur may be in an even better position to seize additional opportunities through subsequent ventures. If the drive to start the second venture was to show others that the first venture's success was the product of skill rather than luck, then that type of entrepreneur may not have satisfied that drive.

If the first success is followed by a failure, then the way the entrepreneur handles the failure may provide insight into what makes that serial entrepreneur tick. Again, if the entrepreneur looks at the failure objectively and learns from the experience, then that is a healthy response. This type of entrepreneur may try again. If the entrepreneur uses various defense mechanisms to rationalize the failure and sets out to start another venture, then he may be setting himself for more failures.

Ironically, in Silicon Valley, starting a venture that failed is often considered a rite of passage. Some venture capital firms actually place a premium on entrepreneurs who have failed over those who may have succeeded in their first ventures or who have never started ventures. These venture capital firms value entrepreneurs who have demonstrated their resiliency and have some humility over entrepreneurs who do not have any scar tissue or who have not been battle tested.

If the serial entrepreneur has a healthy mental framework, then he may be able to turn a venture failure into a learning opportunity. The key to the "hot stove rule" is not to avoid the stove. The key is to learn how to use the stove without getting burned. If the entrepreneur: (1) is savvy to the realities of the marketplace, (2) approaches the next venture with a better team, (3) has more capital in reserve, (4) has more assurance there are customers in search of a business, and (5) has sustainable competitive advantages, then the entrepreneur should be able to hit the ground running and increase the probability for success.

Most successful serial entrepreneurs have experienced at least one venture failure before their current success. When you ask serial entrepreneurs about an earlier failure, they rarely refer to them as failures. Instead, they refer to them as "ventures that didn't work out." While most people would accept their defeat, real entrepreneurs view them as learning experiences and get back in the saddle. Like Thomas Edison, they are quick to note what they learned. In Edison's case, he learned what didn't work in his effort to develop a light bulb. Their focus on finding a solution to a problem as well as sensing and seizing current and future opportunities keeps them from dwelling on the past.

Mentally healthy people recognize that if they want to succeed, then they will need to change the way they approach the ever-changing world. People with mental disorders are not that perceptive or flexible. Instead of learning they expect the world to change. Some of these people spend their lives trying to start ventures that are destined to fail. They keep approaching the entrepreneurial stove without the proper mental framework, attitude, skills, resources, and so forth. In many cases, their compulsive behavior does not stop with their first, second, or even third bankruptcy. They are the epitome of Einstein's definition of insanity.

Successful serial entrepreneurs and multipreneurs recognize the need to adapt to changing conditions. People with mental disorders are not very flexible. Instead of learning from their experiences, they expect *the world* to change. Mentally healthy people change the way they approach the world as it changes.

At What Point Does Entrepreneurism Become an Addiction?

Some serial entrepreneurs feel compelled to start businesses. Some serial entrepreneurs want to change and are able to do so. Some serial entrepreneurs want to change but don't. Some serial entrepreneurs just don't want to change. Some serial entrepreneurs find the process of starting one venture after another to be like an opiate. It provides them with such an intense mental adrenaline rush that they cannot imagine what life would be like if they were not actively starting ventures. Serial entrepreneurs who get to the point that they cannot handle life "between startups" may have a mental disorder.

What drives serial entrepreneurs to start subsequent businesses also indicates whether they have a mental disorder. If serial entrepreneurs start ventures to seize opportunities and are able to maintain a healthy work/life balance, then that may not be a mental disorder. If they sell their ventures and do not want to retire at that time then it may be quite logical for them to start another venture. If the desire to start subsequent ventures is directed to pursuing an untapped market opportunity, then their behavior can be considered logical.

Most entrepreneurs thrive when facing a challenge. If the entrepreneur is like Karl Wallenda and feels most alive when starting a venture, then that may not be a sign of a mental disorder. If, however, the desire to start a subsequent venture is driven by the unwillingness or lack of desire to do anything else, then that may be a sign of a mental disorder. Entrepreneurs who are totally unidimensional and cannot find any other source of satisfaction or sense of identity in their lives when they are "in between startups" may have a mental disorder. While friends and family may encourage them to get a life; unidimensional serial entrepreneurs consider starting ventures to be their life!

Serial entrepreneurs may have one or more mental disorders if they are driven to start businesses because they: (1) just cannot concentrate on one business, (2) want to avoid certain aspects of their personal lives, (3) want to prove others were wrong in their assessment of them, or (4) need a business to provide a vehicle to continue their neuroses.

Some entrepreneurs start subsequent ventures merely because someone gave them an offer for their business they couldn't refuse. Some entrepreneurs sell their business when things are going well because they are concerned about the future success of their ventures. Most serial entrepreneurs plan to sell their ventures so they can start subsequent ventures. They are *deliberate* serial entrepreneurs. The people who do not have a deliberate plan to be serial entrepreneurs may become serial entrepreneurs by default. They look for a new venture to start when they no longer have a venture.

If the entrepreneur's first venture was successful, then the desire to start another venture maybe a natural path to follow and should not be considered a mental disorder. It is interesting to see what these entrepreneurs do when they have free time and the money they received from selling their ventures. Some entrepreneurs look for a new venture opportunity right away. They are like some of the soldiers who have been in combat who reenlist as soon as their tour of duty is over. They find that nothing can match the adrenaline rush. Like Karl Wallenda, they feel alive when they are at the edge. Most entrepreneurs start ventures so they can build and manage them for an extended period of time. Most serial entrepreneurs, however, seem to enjoy the chase more than the catch.

Some entrepreneurs take early retirement and enjoy it. Other entrepreneurs try retirement and can't take it. They find the silence of retirement to be deafening and quickly begin their search for a new opportunity. George Eastman, who founded what is now known as Eastman Kodak, demonstrated what can happen when a person retires before he or she is ready and does not have anything worthwhile to do. He committed suicide soon after retiring. Supposedly, he left a note that read, "Why wait?" Some entrepreneurs who cash out before they have something to do that provides even a fraction of the thrill they found in starting and managing a venture may share some of Eastman's sense of futility.

Serial Entrepreneurs and Multipreneurs: Attention Deficiency Disorder Syndrome?

Serial entrepreneurism and multipreneurism may not be mental disorders if the desire to start additional ventures is market-driven. If the entrepreneur sees a market opportunity that could be served by starting a venture rather than addressing it with the existing venture, then it may make sense to start a separate venture.

It should be noted that some frustration and waning satisfaction after startup is quite natural and normal. Starting a business not only provides an adrenaline rush, it may also provide an incredible sense of accomplishment and fulfillment. There is a big difference between coming down from the high associated with starting a business and ADD (Attention Deficit Disorder). People with ADD find it is almost impossible to focus on one thing for an extended period of time. Starting and growing a business requires considerable focus, discipline, and perseverance.

The challenges of starting a business are markedly different from the challenges of running a business. As noted earlier, if the entrepreneur lacks the skills to deal with the challenges of growing a business and does not have the time or desire to learn those skills, then it is logical for the entrepreneur to either sell the business or to bring in a general manager to direct the venture's operations. If, however, the desire to start additional ventures is driven by boredom, then it may reflect a mental disorder. If the serial entrepreneur or multipreneur starts feeling like a caged tiger soon after the venture is started, then they may be exhibiting a degree of ADD

People with ADD note that listening to others, being patient, and waiting for things can be a real challenge. Their restlessness, propensity to be distracted, and tendency to interrupt others can make it difficult for entrepreneurs with ADD to start and run a business. ADD is discussed in more depth in chapter five.

Conclusion: Serial Entrepreneurs and Multipreneurs - I Can't Stop Myself!

One of the characteristics of a mental disorder is the inability or unwillingness to change one's behavior. The drive to start businesses may reach the level where the entrepreneur is obsessive and compulsive. Obsessiveness applies to situations where an individual just cannot stop thinking about something. Entrepreneurs are frequently cited for their passion. Yet obsessiveness goes well beyond passion. It can be a fixation that inhibits one's ability to think about anything else. While obsessiveness pertains to one's thoughts, compulsiveness pertains to one's behavior. Compulsiveness is reflected in the feeling that you always *must* do something. The next chapter profiles the effects of OCD (Obsessive-Compulsive Disorder) and other mental disorders on entrepreneurism.

An anonymous serial entrepreneur noted, "Entrepreneurship is a disease. It's the worst disease you can have. It can't be cured and you die with it." He noted that entrepreneurs cannot rest because they are always thinking about ideas for what can be done or done better. They are cursed with the belief that there is always "a better way." He also noted that the never-ending drive to find a better way makes it difficult for them to work for someone else. Most firms "settle" for "good enough" or have an "If it isn't broke, then don't fix it." mentality.

People who operate with an entrepreneurial mindset are driven to find better ways to do things and better things to do. This often produces head-on collisions with established practices, standard operating procedures, and "not-invented here" attitudes which ignore or even punish people who come up with better ways - especially truly innovative ways.

Entrepreneurs who are obsessed with seizing opportunities and feel compelled to start businesses to capitalize on them are like moths driven to a flame. They just cannot stop themselves. They cannot turn their entrepreneurism off. They cannot relax when they spend time with friends and family. They cannot slow down. They cannot retire. To outsiders, they seem to be cursed; to them it is what they do … It is irresistible. The only way they can deal with their anxiety is to start another business.

Richard Branson observed, "Business opportunities are like buses, there is always one coming." When Brett Martin, founder of Castle Branch Inc., was asked what he would do if he was to step down from being CEO or sell his shares, he responded he would take the weekend off and then start another business. He also commented that he had seen and related to the "So many bars and so little time!" t-shirt when his board of directors had its meeting in Key West.

Being a serial entrepreneur or a multipreneur is like most things in life. Their behavior can be constructive and rewarding, or their behavior can be destructive and harmful. It all depends on how the entrepreneur handles starting additional ventures. The process and challenges associated with starting businesses are like "the thrill of the hunt." They can identify with Karl Wallenda's comment about being alive when he was "on the wire." If the entrepreneur is successful, handles the inevitable setbacks in a constructive manner, and develops and maintains a work-life balance, then the "hunt" can beneficial.

Many entrepreneurs miss the ventures they started when they sell them. If the entrepreneur experiences serious and lasting "post-partum depression" while he/she is "between" ventures," then the entrepreneur may be even more motivated to start another business. This could be risky if the new venture is started without sufficient due diligence. One serial entrepreneur noted that when he was "between ventures" he felt like a drug addict going through withdrawal looking for methadone to ease the pain!

Being a serial entrepreneur or multipreneur can also have detrimental consequences for the entrepreneur's business. If the serial entrepreneur is so antsy to start the next business, then he/she may not take the time to develop a successor and/or the systems needed to run his current business.

Being a serial entrepreneur or multipreneur can also cause collateral damage for others in his/her life. The entrepreneur's commitment to one or more ventures limits time for one's family. It also limits time for hobbies, which can be useful in reducing stress by diverting one's attention from the various anxiety-producing issues. The fixation on one's business can also lead to unhealthy eating habits and the lack of exercise.

In extreme cases, the pursuit of additional ventures may be a mental disorder. Who knows, the inability of serial entrepreneurs and multipreneurs to control themselves may lead to the creation of a television show called *Entrepreneurial Interventions* that profiles the challenges of exorcising the "entrepreneurial demons."

For some entrepreneurs, there will never be enough time to start all the businesses they would like to start or enough startups to satisfy them. The next chapter focuses on mental disorders and what can be done to address the disorders.

> *"This is my last startup ... really."*
> Anonymous serial entrepreneur

Chapter Five

HELPING ENTREPRENEURS COPE WITH THEIR CHALLENGES

*"Some people hear their own inner voices ... with great clearness ...
and they live by what they hear. Such people become crazy ...
or they become legends."*
The opening lines from the film, *Legends of the Fall*[18]
based on the novella by Jim Harrison

We live in a time when there appears to be a support group for almost every type of personal challenge or malady. There are support groups for gamblers, drinkers, smokers, adulterers, widows/widowers, and so forth. A search of the Internet using the words *entrepreneurs* and *anonymous* revealed numerous organizations and articles. One organization has even trademarked Entrepreneurs Anonymous®.

The multitude of electronic links may indicate the need entrepreneurs may have for assistance in coping with their psychological challenges. For example, one web site helps people operate "under the radar" while at work so their employers will not discover they are planning their entrepreneurial escape. This group may not be the only group that wants to keep their entrepreneurial desires hidden.

Numerous people are so fearful of how others including their friends and family will react to their desire to be an entrepreneur that they keep their desires a secret. In a sense, they are afraid to *come out* of the "entrepreneurism closet." They do not believe the people close to them – including one's spouse – can understand why they would take such a risk.

As noted earlier, the U.S. Small Business Administration estimates that about a third of all Americans between the ages of 20 and 65 are thinking about starting a business. That's nearly 50 million people. Yet only one million businesses are started each year - including those started by serial entrepreneurs and multipreneurs. This means less than two percent of the people who are thinking about starting a business will actually start one this year. This demonstrates that the fear of failure may be stronger than the fear of missing an opportunity.

The question should be raised, "Is the desire to be an entrepreneur grounds for one's spouse to seek a divorce?" Many *normal* people consider starting a business as being reckless with the family's finances and future. Can one's preoccupation with starting a venture be considered an irreconcilable difference and/or emotional incompatibility? Can starting a business be considered spousal or familial abandonment or abuse? Can starting a business be considered comparable to having an adulterous affair? One spouse's comment about her husband's entrepreneurial pursuits put it in an interesting context when she said, "At least it's not another woman."

One web site helps people get over their desire to be an entrepreneur by encouraging them to contact the former spouses of failed entrepreneurs and people who had co-signed loans for entrepreneurs. The site also recommends reading the legal notices profiling bankruptcies and visiting debtors in prison.

Most entrepreneurs believe that only entrepreneurs can understand entrepreneurs. Being an entrepreneur can be a very lonely existence. Having a support group of like-minded people who can empathize with their concerns can help them. Having a "sponsor" to call when they are on the brink of falling off the wagon by having entrepreneurial thoughts may also help a "recovering" serial entrepreneur or multipreneur keep from having a relapse when they have the urge to start another venture.

Helping Entrepreneurs Cope With Their Situations: Is There a Cure?

Three questions can now be raised. First, "Can a person who really wants to be an entrepreneur be convinced not to be an entrepreneur?" Second, "Should you try to convince a person who really wants to be an entrepreneur to not be an entrepreneur?" Third, "Can the demon that drives the obsessiveness be exorcised or is it impossible to be a *reformed* serial entrepreneur or multipreneur?"

The following four questions may be more appropriate. First, "Can the irresistible desire to start a business be channeled into some other type of endeavor?" Second, "Can anything replace the feeling they get from seizing the entrepreneurial opportunity?" Third, "Can becoming an angel investor, a venture capitalist, or an adjunct professor at the nearest business school so one can talk about entrepreneurship be enough to displace the obsession?" Fourth, "Is starting another venture the only fix for their addiction?"

One serial entrepreneur noted that he was a "recovering" entrepreneur. He stated, "I've been on the wagon. I haven't started a business in five years!" He was quick to note that it had not been easy. He truly missed projecting when the venture would get traction, setting up beta sites, figuring capitalization and valuation, calculating the burn rate, and doing "deals."

Alcoholics Anonymous® uses what is known as the Serenity Prayer to help its members meet the challenges associated with their addiction. Serial entrepreneurs and multipreneurs who are obsessed with gaps in the market and feel compelled to start businesses to fill them may find the following prayer helpful:

The Serenity Prayer for Entrepreneurs

*"God grant me the serenity
to accept that I cannot seize every market opportunity,
the courage to pursue the opportunities others cannot see, and
the wisdom to not let others know what I am doing until I succeed.
Let me live one day at a time without being preoccupied with
all the opportunities that I will not be able to seize."*

Mental health depends a lot on self-awareness and one's self-concept. One's perceptions and attitudes have a considerable impact on one's behavior. Entrepreneurs who are willing to take an objective look at their behavior are more likely to modify their behavior so it will to lead to more favorable results. They will also be better off if they surround themselves with people who provide useful feedback and demonstrate personal and professional balance.

Serial entrepreneurs and multipreneurs need to recognize what drives them. Some serial entrepreneurs and multipreneurs are so compulsive that they cannot help themselves. If they are truly addicted and their behavior is having detrimental personal consequences, then they need to get professional help. Yet some serial entrepreneurs and multipreneurs do not want to change.

When I asked a psychotherapist what it would take for a person to have a major personality change, she noted it would take at least two one-hour sessions per week for about two years. She also noted that the person would have to want to change from the very beginning of the sessions. Psychologist Morris Massey noted that most people must have a "significant emotional event" in their lives to have a marked and lasting change in how they see the world and how they behave in it. The question then is, "What will it take for a compulsive serial entrepreneur or multipreneur to be truly committed to changing his/her life?" Will it take a heart attack, divorce and/or bankruptcy? In many cases one or more of these may not be enough for lasting change to take place.

Which is worse: Being an Entrepreneur or Being an Employee?

Which is worse, taking the risk of pursuing your entrepreneurial dream or working for someone else and not pursuing your dream? Granted, there are things that can make being an entrepreneur difficult, but working for someone else - being an "employee" - can also be a source of great frustration. Most people who do not like their jobs do not like their lives.

Life is different when you are an entrepreneur. You may have to mortgage your home, take money from your equity line, cash in your retirement plans, and withhold contributions to your kids' 529 college funds to start your business and/or to cover cash shortfalls. You can't take worry-free vacations if you even take vacations. You cannot enjoy a good night's sleep because numerous issues about your business keep you awake or wake you up. You don't know what quality time with your spouse is like, what is really going on in your kids' lives, what extra-curricular activities are like, what pleasure reading is like or what hobbies are like.

One entrepreneur noted that she was on the receiving end of too many "We're not in that business." or "It's up to R&D to come up with new ideas – not you." when she suggested innovative ideas where she worked. One of the most telling deterrents to innovative and/or entrepreneurial thinking in established firms is, "The last person who came up with an idea like that – doesn't work here anymore!"

Ironically, most companies are created by people who are dissatisfied with their employers. When a number of their ideas disappear into a black hole, never to be seen again, they quit and start their own firms – often as competitors of their former employer.

Even entrepreneurs who build solid management teams, develop performance-enhancing systems and master the art of delegation rarely get a chance to catch their breath and recharge their batteries. There is always something – or more likely, a lot of things – that need to be addressed.

Unlike salaried people, even senior level executives, it is difficult for an entrepreneur to turn the "stuff" switch off when leaving the office – it is always there. A venture capitalist noted, "The challenges entrepreneurs face are relentless."

You can't mentally walk away from being an entrepreneur at the end of the day. There are fires to be put out or prevented. Immediate issues need to be balanced with future issues. There are opportunities to improve the business to be explored and analyzed. There are decisions to be made and implemented. One entrepreneur demonstrated an upbeat and healthy attitude, however, when he said, "I am in the solutions business. My job is to make good things happen."

One entrepreneur noted, "You would have to be a masochist to bring so much frustration and pain into your life." Another entrepreneur noted, "You'd have to be crazy to start a business that has to deal with all the bureaucracy and the idiots out there who work for the government."

Being an entrepreneur can be lonely because you are so exposed. Harry Truman's "The buck stops here." applies equally well for entrepreneurs. Gene Haley, founder of Wilmington Pharmaceuticals, echoed Truman's observation when he stated, "When you work for a corporation, you can always complain about how bad your boss is. When you are an entrepreneur, 'you' are the boss."

There are two other drawbacks associated with giving up the corporate life to start a business. You give up having support staffs to assist you. You also lose having access to funds without having to constantly seek them from outside sources. In the beginning, you are the support staff, and you are on your own in seeking funding.

Yet in spite of all the drawbacks, few career paths can bring the adrenaline high associated with being an entrepreneur. Entrepreneurs face a never-ending set of issues that challenge their creativity, resourcefulness and perseverance. When they are in "the zone" they are like a finely-tuned car that is firing on all cylinders. They are like Karl Wallenda when he was on the wire.

Real entrepreneurs are meant to start ventures - it is who they are. It is not in their nature to stay on the sidelines as spectators - when the world is full of opportunities that need to be seized. The statement that ships are meant to be sailed – not to rest at anchor in a safe harbor – applies to entrepreneurs. The following poem captures some of what drives entrepreneurs to seize opportunities. The phrase in the title has been attributed to many people, but this poem's author (probably British given the spelling of harbor) is unknown.

Ships Are Safe in the Harbour

"All I live for is now
All I stand for is where and how
All I wish for are magic moments

As I sail through change
My resolve remains the same
What I chose are magic moments

Because ships are safe in the harbour
But that is not what ships are made for
The mind could stretch much further
But it seems that is not what our minds are trained for

We call for random order
You can't control Mother nature's daughter

Ships are safe in the harbour
But that is not what ships are built for

The witch hunter roams
The scary thing is that he's not alone
He's trying to down my magic moments

As we sail through change
Ride the wind of a silent rage
And sing laments of magic moments"

A Closer Look at Mental Disorders

It is time to take a closer look at whether the qualities that characterize entrepreneurism may be considered mental disorders. A note of caution, however, needs to be provided here. This book is not intended to be the bible or to even scratch the surface of the nature and treatment of mental disorders. It is merely intended to highlight certain types of behavior that may affect entrepreneurial behavior. *The Diagnostic and Statistical Manual of Mental Disorders* identifies numerous mental disorders. People who want to learn more about mental disorders are encouraged to read the latest edition.

Chapter two profiled the normal to insanity continuum. The continuum indicated that most behavior – even idiosyncrasies – is within the sphere of normalcy. It is only when one's behavior is extreme and has detrimental consequences that it is considered a mental disorder or even a mental illness. The rest of this chapter takes a closer look at certain behaviors that may be exhibited by entrepreneurs and whether they are idiosyncrasies or mental disorders.

Can Being Overly Optimistic be a Mental Disorder?

Real entrepreneurs are optimistic and opportunistic. They believe they can make good things happen. They believe in their self-efficacy. Their optimism comes from a sense of well-being. They believe they can change reality by changing the possibilities, probabilities and, in some cases, the states of nature.

Real entrepreneurs are optimistic even in bad times. They also don't wait for the economy to turn around. They may know that seventy percent of new ventures fail, but they do not think that statistic applies to them.

Real entrepreneurs welcome the challenge. They have a "Bring it on" attitude. They don't wait to be asked or invited. They take the initiative. They are willing to step into darkness when the future is uncertain and make intuitive leaps when solid information is not available to them.

Steve Jobs may have found the "sweet spot" between confidence and arrogance when he envisioned the opportunities for innovative products.* He noted on numerous occasions that he did not do conventional market research. His reasons included that he had such a great group of people working at Apple - especially in the new product development team - that Apple developed products they would like. He reasoned that if they liked the product, consumers would as well. He also noted that consumers can't identify products they would like if they can't even imagine them.

Real entrepreneurs are also driven to seize opportunities. Ambiguity and complexity cause most people to back away. Real entrepreneurs thrive in ambiguous and complex situations. They experiment, test hypotheses, discover, launch, and learn.

---

*I refer to Steve Jobs a lot in this book. This is because his accomplishments and idiosyncrasies are fairly well known. Also, his behavior is very fresh in my mind because I just finished teaching two classes about him.

Yet there are times when an entrepreneur's optimism may have negative consequences. There are times when being more of a realist is in order. Entrepreneurs who make commitments that cannot be honored run the risk of not only losing sales and clients; they also run the risk of being blackballed. Supposedly, Bill Gates signed a contract to deliver an operating system to IBM early in his entrepreneurial journey. Yet he did not have an operating system at the time. If he had not been able to purchase a system for $50,000 from another firm, then Microsoft might not be the firm that it is today, and Bill Gates may not have become one of the world's wealthiest individuals. Often, there is a fine line between success and failure - a little luck may make the difference.

Many entrepreneurs have a "What the hell, I can always start over if it doesn't work out." attitude. This carefree attitude can cause them to be careless. Being overly optimistic may cause entrepreneurs to not look before they leap or to do due diligence. It may cause entrepreneurs to be blind to certain realities and to not do necessary reality checks when caution is needed.

Being overly optimistic and arrogant often go hand in hand. Wisdom involves knowing what you can and cannot do. People who are arrogant are either unaware of their shortcomings or choose to ignore them. Most successful entrepreneurs factor Murphy's Law into their decision processes. Murphy's Law states, "Anything that can go wrong will go wrong – and at the most inopportune time." Wisdom often means not taking unnecessary risks. People who are arrogant do not believe Murphy's Law applies to them. While being overly optimistic may not be an "official" mental disorder, it can be fatal.

Arrogant entrepreneurs do not handle negativism and/or when things do not go as planned. Steve Jobs was known for attacking people who said something could not be done. Arrogant people are quick to take credit for successes. Yet they are not willing to accept the responsibility when things do not work out. They tend to blame the lack of success on external factors.

Arrogant people also fail to conduct what the army calls "after action reviews" to learn why things worked and/or did not work out. This keeps them from developing a pool of lessons learned which would contribute to them doing better in the future.

Serial entrepreneurs who are arrogant tend to ignore reality, not collect relevant information, and not seek others' advice. As noted earlier, their arrogance often produces an, "I've already made up my mind don't confuse me with the facts." attitude.

Paranoia: A Little Bit can be Helpful

Paranoia may play a role in entrepreneurism. Paranoia can be manifested in numerous ways. In some cases, it may actually have a positive impact on a business. A moderate level of paranoia keeps you on your toes. It also reduces arrogance and complacency. Paranoia can keep an entrepreneur from taking customers, competitors, and success for granted. Andy Grove, co-founder of Intel, captured the value of having a little paranoia in his book, *Only the Paranoid Survive*. When Jeff Bezos was asked on *60 Minutes* about all the challenges Amazon faces he noted, "I tell people around here to wake up petrified and afraid every morning."[19]

Paranoia can be debilitating if it goes beyond moderation. People with paranoia tend to see conspirators at every turn. Entrepreneurs who fear that someone may be trying to take their idea or their venture's success away exhibit symptoms of paranoia. Some entrepreneurs are so afraid someone is going to steal their ideas, client list, and so forth that they become highly secretive. Withholding information and being suspicious of every employee's intentions can jeopardize the business and cause good people to quit.

Yet a more subtle form of paranoia is the tendency for some entrepreneurs to feel very uncomfortable when things are going well. Instead of savoring the moment, they adopt a "Things are going to too well ... something must go wrong" mental state. These entrepreneurs live in the shadow of Murphy's Law. This type of paranoia can keep an entrepreneur from planning for the future.

Entrepreneurs need to spend some of their time running "What if ... ?" scenarios about potential threats so they can reduce the likelihood of being blindsided. They also need to develop contingency plans for events that may occur. Yet if they spend all their time running scenarios and developing contingency plans they will not be focusing enough on running their ventures – which, in turn, may increase their firm's vulnerability.

Entrepreneurs who are convinced something bad is about to happen tend to focus their attention to looking over their shoulders. They avoid almost anything that has the potential to go wrong. They also are reluctant to make long-term commitments. Their behavior is similar to people who have agoraphobia, which is sometimes called the fear of "leaving home" syndrome. They are afraid to leave a safe place. They are like people who check the locks on their doors two or three times before going to bed and then stay awake all night listening for strange noises. Before long, the lack of sleep keeps them from recharging their mental and physical batteries. This further accentuates their inability to meet the various challenges the next day will bring.

For a business to grow and succeed, opportunities must be seized, decisions must be made, resources must be committed to the firm's future, and certain risks must be accepted. Before moving on, I cannot resist including Joseph Heller's perspective of paranoia in his book, *Catch 22*. He noted, "Just because you're paranoid doesn't mean they aren't after you."

Being Obsessive and Compulsive in Moderation may be Beneficial

Obsessiveness and compulsiveness are the two areas that come up most when people describe peculiar entrepreneurial behavior – especially the behavior of serial entrepreneurs and multipreneurs. When obsessiveness and compulsiveness are extreme, they are called an obsessive-compulsive disorder (OCD). Yet the obsessiveness and compulsiveness may even be exhibited before a person starts his/her first venture. As noted earlier in the book, some people get so wrapped up in pursuing an idea for a new business that their fixation interferes with almost every aspect of their lives. They can't focus on their jobs, can't sleep, and are so distracted that they shouldn't even be driving a car.

Entrepreneurs live in a world of spinning plates, where there are a multitude of things that affect their businesses. It is easy for entrepreneurs to be distracted and to lose sight of the things that are truly important and that must be done at that time in a certain manner. Obsessiveness can be beneficial if it is directed to the right things and is calibrated, so that it does not keep the entrepreneur from doing other things that need to be done. Obsessiveness can enable a person to have a laser-like focus in a world that is full of distractions.

Steve Jobs exhibited obsessive and compulsive behavior throughout most of his career. He drove his staff crazy with his fixation on certain things – especially simplicity of design and making sure the products were incredible. His preoccupation with how things looked – including the inside of computers – which consumers would never see. Even the colors of things that did not matter much had to be the right shade – what *he* defined as perfect.

Yet without such obsessiveness, Apple would have been like most firms by shipping good products - even really good products - but they would not have been *great* products. Few brands have turned relatively sane consumers into fanatics. Millions of consumers have become obsessive and compulsive in their desire to own Apple products.

Entrepreneurs who recognize they have obsessive and compulsive tendencies should surround themselves with people who will figuratively blow a whistle when the entrepreneur needs to step back. Only then, will the entrepreneur be able to direct his/her attention so it is more balanced and directed to other important and pressing issues. Unfortunately, extreme cases of obsessiveness and compulsiveness are mental disorders that are hard to address. Research has shown that medication and therapy are not very effective for most people with OCD.

Having an Attention Deficit Disorder May Foster Multiple Perspectives

Attention Deficit Disorder (ADD) may be the polar opposite of obsessiveness and compulsiveness. Like obsessiveness and compulsiveness, people can have varying levels of attention deficits. Having a low or even moderate level of attention deficiency can be beneficial. Entrepreneurs who are obsessive and compulsive run the risk of being so focused on one or two things that they miss the need to expand their radar so they can identify and explore emerging opportunities. Steve Jobs noted that when you are on bombing run you don't change targets.[20] This may be true, but you also need to make sure you are considering the right targets before you start the bombing run.

Entrepreneurs who have difficulty focusing on anything for even a nominal amount of time find it hard to manage a venture – especially repetitive and mundane activities. David Neeleman, founder of Jet Blue, noted in an interview on *60 Minutes* how difficult it can be to remain focused. He noted that he has trouble even reading a book with his kids.[21]

There are many situations when entrepreneurs need to be patient and persistent. They need to be able to hang in there when they could be distracted. They cannot afford to be seduced by too many opportunities like the songs of the Sirens in Homer's *Odyssey*. While venture capital firms like entrepreneurs who have passion, they also want entrepreneurs who will be completely dedicated to their ventures. They cannot afford entrepreneurs who are easily distracted.

Entrepreneurs with attention deficit issues are like popcorn poppers. They can generate a lot of ideas because their minds are constantly jumping from one thing to the next. They are like the first stage of brainstorming where the participants are encouraged to generate as many ideas as possible without any evaluation or criticism.

Brainstorming focuses on the quantity rather than quality of ideas. Yet in the world of business, ideation needs to be followed by evaluation. It is for this reason that entrepreneurs with attention deficits need to surround themselves with people who can conduct constructive reality checks. This is one of the reasons why entrepreneurs need to have a financial officer and/or advisors who make sure the entrepreneur does not make commitments beyond the firm's funding.

People frequently consider ADD to be the same as Attention Deficit Hyperactivity Disorder (ADHD). One of the major differences between them is the level of activity exhibited by the person. People with ADD are easily distracted. People with ADHD are hyperactive and easily distracted. Their hyperactivity makes it even more difficult for them to interact with people. They have trouble waiting for people – even to the point of waiting for people to complete their sentences. Their restlessness may also prompt them to be impulsive. The propensity for serial entrepreneurs to get caught up in planning their next ventures has another drawback. The phrase, "Life is what happens while you are making plans." applies to people with ADD and ADHD.

It is important for people, however, to recognize there is a major difference between being highly motivated and hyperactive. People who are passionate about something do not have a lot of patience. They want to make things happen and have little patience for bureaucracy and following protocol. Entrepreneurs who are restless and want to make things happen right now do not necessarily have ADHD. Entrepreneurs by their very nature are proactive. Their drive to change the world – and to do it now should not be considered a form of ADHD.

Dyslexia: It Can be Great for Creativity but Not Necessarily Great for Managing

People with dyslexia process information differently. If thinking differently and connecting "the dots" enhance creativity, then dyslexia may be beneficial. A study by the Cass Business School in London found that fifteen percent of the population is dyslexic. Certain aspects of ADD are similar to dyslexia when it comes to starting and managing a business. The Cass Business School study also that found that thirty-five percent of the entrepreneurs admitted to being dyslexic. Norm Brodsy noted in *Inc. Magazine* that the study should have also asked entrepreneurs if they have ADD. He believes the number would be close to ninety percent.[22]

If the entrepreneur can channel or even focus on the issues that enhance success, then being dyslexic may not be detrimental. If one's dyslexia interferes with the processing of key information, then it may be detrimental. Most people with dyslexia tend to have difficulty handling details. Entrepreneurs who are dyslexic - like entrepreneurs who have ADD - need to have a good support staff to delegate some of the decisions to and who will oversee the implementation of the decisions. This may actually strengthen their firms by engaging their people more than entrepreneurs who have a tendency to micromanage.

Dyslexia may have another benefit. Entrepreneurs frequently need to be resourceful in their efforts to find solutions to challenging situations. Life can be rather chaotic for people who are dyslexic. Because they usually don't do things the way most people do things, they spend their lives creating ways to make things work for them. They also have to learn how to handle setbacks. This contributes to their perseverance and resilience – two important qualities for entrepreneurs. Various sources list Leonardo Da Vinci, Albert Einstein, Henry Ford, and Eli Whitney as having dyslexia.

Idiosyncrasies and Mental Disorders: One Size Doesn't Fit All Entrepreneurs

It would be too simplistic and stereotypical to say all entrepreneurs are the same. That also applies to their idiosyncrasies and possible mental disorders. Many entrepreneurs are hybrids. They may have a combination of idiosyncrasies. Their tendency to see things differently and to behave differently makes them stand out from the crowd.

Their contempt for the status quo and desire to find better ways to do things and better things to do, causes them to break the rules or feel the rules do not apply to them. Larry Page and Sergey Brin changed the way the IPO game is played when they went against tradition and launched Google's IPO as an auction. They took the underwriters out of the equation.

Some people offer an interesting way of explaining entrepreneurial behavior. They believe that to understand an entrepreneur you should study juvenile delinquents. Juvenile delinquents want to do things their way – even if it means breaking the rules. Many young entrepreneurs identify with Ferris Bueller when he took his infamous day off from high school. The line from the movie, "Hey Cameron. You realize if we played by the rules right now we'd be in gym?" captures Ferris's attitude and philosophy.

Steve Jobs may have been the epitome of this type of behavior. He didn't believe the rules applied to him. He used his "reality distortion field" to bend or redefine reality to fit his needs. In many cases, he and his people made what others considered impossible possible.

Like juvenile delinquents, many entrepreneurs think and operate outside the box – if they even see the box. Numerous well-known entrepreneurs were college drop outs. They saw opportunities and did not want to let them pass them by. They wanted to seize the opportunity by seizing the moment. Bill Gates, Steve Jobs, Michael Dell, and Mark Zuckerberg were drop outs. Jerry Yang and David Filo were graduate students when they dropped out to create Yahoo. A few years later, Sergey Brin and Larry Page dropped out of graduate school to create Google.

Being a drop out is not limited to college students. Jeff Bezos was a corporate dropout when he left a very successful financial career on Wall Street to ride the e-commerce tsunami. In 1994 at the age of 30, he came across a report projecting annual growth in Internet commerce to be 2300 percent. He noted that nothing outside a petri dish grows that rapidly.[23]

Quitting his job may have seemed like he was taking a big risk, but what made his behavior even more noteworthy and crazy to *normal* people is that he did so without knowing what type of business he would start or where he would start it. He told the movers to follow him as he headed west. He told the movers he would let them know the destination when he figured it out. While many people considered him to be crazy to give up so much, he thought he would be crazy *not to pursue* the opportunity in what he considered to be a critical "category-changing time."[24]

Webster's Dictionary defines mania as an abnormal degree or excess of something. The terms hypomania, narcissism, megalomania, messianic, omniscient, and omnipotence frequently come up in describing the mindsets and resulting behavior for some entrepreneurs. Each of these terms describes the tendency to exhibit an abnormal amount of a particular type of behavior. These conditions combine some of the conditions profiled earlier in this chapter.

People who have hypomania tend to be arrogant. Their arrogance can make it difficult for them to work with other people. They also tend to lack the social skills and/or patience needed to get along with other people. It is interesting to note that when Steve Jobs was asked why he did not make the effort to develop more favorable relationships with his people, he stated that he might have been able to be nicer but that it wasn't his nature. He also noted that he was not sure his people would have been able to do so many great things if he had been nicer.

Entrepreneurs with hypomania tend to see every moment spent doing something not related to their businesses to be a moment they lost that could have been invested in their businesses. People who are hypomanic also tend to stand out because they do not sleep much. It's not because they worry about things. They do not sleep because they want to make things happen and sleep keeps them from doing the things that need to be done. When a young entrepreneur was asked what kept him up at 2:00 a.m., he responded, "Not my girlfriend. I was so caught up in my business that she moved out because I would not pay enough attention to her."

People with hypomania are like children in some respects. Anyone who has tried to get a child to take a nap knows how hard it is. Taking a nap to a child is like turning off the world. To most adults, taking a nap does not have much of an opportunity cost. Their lives are not as new and exciting. The same also applies to having an upbeat attitude. Most kids have not had as many setbacks as adults, so they seem to have an upbeat attitude. People who are hypomanic, like kids, seem to have more energy than most adults.

Some entrepreneurs exhibit narcissistic behavior. Margaret Heffernan, author of *Willful Blindness*, raised some interesting points about people who have narcissistic tendencies in her article, "How to Survive Working for a Narcissistic Leader." She noted the following characteristics and consequences of narcissistic leaders:[25]

1. Times of great change require leaders who have immense vision, courage, and the capacity to ignore what everyone else is doing.
2. Psychoanalysts describe narcissistic personalities as independent, innovative, and drawn to power and glory.

3. Narcissists are sometimes great leaders because they have vision and are sufficiently self-absorbed not to care (or even notice) how mad they may appear to others. They rarely suffer from doubt or second thoughts and can come across as very aggressive.
4. Their extreme absorption in their own vision blinds them to risks, problems or nuance. Being part of their ride can be exhilarating, instructive, inspiring and lucrative. But hanging on for that ride is emotionally and professionally taxing.
5. If their vision is wrong, they'll lead everyone over the cliff and never notice. The other problem is that, while their interpersonal skills are poor, they will take all dissent personally.
6. Accept that narcissists have no desire to change. Even if they're wreaking havoc, they won't care. They know they're right. If you think you can change them, you're wrong, will waste time - and endure a lot of abuse along the way.
7. The tragedy of narcissists, of course, is that having defeated a mighty foe or delivered epic change, they are the very last people to enjoy the fruits of their labor. If you let them, they'll destroy what they've built.

People who have megalomania are characterized by delusional fantasies. Their fantasies can be in various areas. People with megalomania may be so bold as to believe they can save the world. I do not know how many entrepreneurs believe they can *save* the world, but many set out to *change* the world. Henry Ford was so focused on making automobiles with internal combustion engines affordable for the masses that he was considered a monomaniac on a mission.

Messianic behavior may seem like an extreme case of hypomania and megalomania. People who are messianic act as if they are on a crusade. Steve Jobs exhibited this behavior when he launched the Macintosh in 1984 with the famous 1984 ad that was aired during the Super Bowl. Steve Jobs considered himself to be "the last force of freedom." The ad captured the anti "Big Brother" attitude portrayed by George Orwell's book, *1984*. The ad portrayed IBM as Big Brother which controlled people's behavior. The ad noted that with the Macintosh, 1984 would not be like the 1984 portrayed in Orwell's book. If you haven't seen the ad, then check it out on YouTube. It may be one of the greatest ads ever.

Omniscience and omnipotence are very unusual conditions. The Random House Unabridged Dictionary defines omniscient as, "Having complete or unlimited knowledge, awareness, or understanding." People with this condition believe they know it all. Omnipotence is often called the God Complex. People with this condition think they can accomplish anything they want. Entrepreneurs with either or both of these conditions can be so egocentric that they are delusional. They tend to drive people away with their "My way or the highway" attitude. They also tend to underestimate the risks associated with their endeavors. In almost all cases, reality proves they are not as smart as they think and/or they do not control the world.

Conclusion: Can The Entrepreneurial Drive be Cured? Should it be Cured?

This chapter started by defining a mental disorder as behavior that is extreme and has detrimental consequences. It noted that when the behavior is very dysfunctional, it could be a form of mental illness. It noted that most idiosyncrasies are not the same as mental disorders. Many of the idiosyncrasies profiled in this chapter may actually be beneficial if they are exhibited in moderation.

This book has also noted that entrepreneurs like hanging out with other entrepreneurs because it usually takes an entrepreneur to understand another entrepreneur. Three statements capture how entrepreneurs may be seen. First, "You're only crazy in the eyes of *normal* people, other entrepreneurs consider you to be fairly normal." Second, "You only stand out when you are outside the asylum!" Third, "What appears to be crazy to other people is quite sane to the person doing it."

As noted earlier, entrepreneurs like Steve Jobs and Fred Smith were considered crazy by most people when they launched companies to sell "personal" computers and deliver parcels almost anywhere in the world. In their minds they were not crazy because they envisioned where the world was going and had the courage of their convictions to start businesses that have changed the world.

"If they weren't entrepreneurs, they'd be cocaine junkies."
Anonymous venture capitalist

Epilogue

THANK GOODNESS FOR ENTREPRENEURS

If you look up the definition of crazy in Webster's Dictionary you will find "a nonconforming person." If entrepreneurs conformed to what is the norm, then who would challenge the status quo and conventional wisdom? Their personality quirks and idiosyncrasies – if in moderation and appropriately channeled – can be the source of creativity and innovation. If entrepreneurs conformed to what is the norm, then who would create the ventures that develop breakthrough products, services, processes and business models.

The classic line from the movie *When Harry Met Sally* shows how *normal* people often envy the freedom and courage exhibited by entrepreneurs. In the film when Meg Ryan exhibits a certain type of behavior (which would be hard to describe here) in a restaurant, a lady at another table tells the waitress, "I'll have what she's having."

It seems appropriate as I wrap up this book to highlight a few of the attitudes and corresponding behaviors that separate entrepreneurs from *normal* people. The list is far from exhaustive, but is does profile some of the qualities that, if more people adopted them, would make the world a more interesting and better place.

Noteworthy Entrepreneurial Qualities

- Entrepreneurs welcome the challenge. They have a "Bring it on" attitude.

- Entrepreneurs take the initiative, they don't wait to be asked or invited.

- Entrepreneurs are willing to step into the darkness.

- Entrepreneurs are willing to make intuitive leaps.

- Entrepreneurs thrive in times of discontinuity and ambiguity.

- Entrepreneurs create new products, processes, business models, markets, and industries.

- Entrepreneurs disrupt markets and industries by creating chaos for established firms.

If entrepreneurs didn't live with the mantra "There has to be a better way." then they wouldn't have the perseverance and resilience needed to handle the setbacks in their quest to improve the way we work and live. Niccolo Machiavelli wrote in his book *The Prince*, "There is nothing more dangerous to take in hand, more perilous to conduct, or more uncertain in its success, than to take the lead in the introduction of a new order of things."

The entrepreneur's drive to seize an opportunity without a safety net should be commended rather than questioned. George Bernard Shaw observed, "Reasonable people adapt themselves to the world. Unreasonable people attempt to adapt the world to them. All progress, therefore, depends on unreasonable people." If entrepreneurism is not normal, then maybe we all need to be a bit *less normal*.

We live in a world full of naysayers, skeptics, Monday morning quarterbacks, and managers who have been the basis for the *Dilbert* comic strip. We need people who are able to operate at the "entrepreneurial edge." Successful entrepreneurs turn dreams into reality. Their optimistic, "We can make it happen" attitude is contagious and refreshing. They bring innovation to the marketplace and they punish mediocrity. They challenge the status quo and force larger, more established firms to get their acts together. In some respects, they actually help established firms by keeping them from being complacent and taking customers for granted.

Entrepreneurism should be encouraged and revered. Their courage to boldly go where no one has gone may be America's greatest competitive advantage. After writing this book I believe George Bernard Shaw would have been more accurate if he stressed our society's need for *reasonably* unreasonable men and women.

A closer look at entrepreneurism reveals it may not be a mental disorder. For that matter, most serial entrepreneurs and multipreneurs do not have mental disorders. The desire to start one or more ventures is not a mental disorder, unless it has a truly detrimental effect on the entrepreneur's life and the entrepreneur is unwilling or unable to change. Awareness of the need to change and the ability to change are the hallmarks of mental health. Every entrepreneur has personal idiosyncrasies. Many of the personal qualities associated with entrepreneurism have the potential to be mental disorders if they are taken to their extreme.

This book started with the "Are you crazy?" question people are asked when they embark on the entrepreneurial journey. Maybe entrepreneurs are the ones who are the *most* sane. Most people live non-Wallenda lives. Most people dream dreams but seldom act on them. Most people wonder what life would have been like if they had stepped out of their comfort zone and seized the moment. Most people have resigned themselves to the fact that work is not supposed to be fulfilling and that life begins at retirement.

Maybe entrepreneurs are not *that* crazy. Maybe the risks associated with starting a venture and the uncertainty about its success are not that great. Maybe the real questions are: (1) "Are entrepreneurs taking greater risks than most people take during their lives?" *Normal* people take risks every day, (2) "Are the risks entrepreneurs take greater than the risk people take when they make a commitment at the alter - a commitment to someone they may have known for less than a year - "to love and cherish until death do you part?", (3) "Are their risks any greater than the risk people take when they have children?", and (4) "Are their risks any greater than the risk people take when they allow their career, mortgage, and livelihood to be influenced by a CEO who may not have the employees' best interests at heart?" When you consider these and the myriad decisions, commitments, and risks *normal* people take on an ongoing basis, then deciding to start a business and have some influence on one's future may not be that crazy.

Steve Jobs was known for closing his presentation of product launches with his "One more thing." I would like to close this book with one more thing. It should be clear by now that entrepreneurs are not normal. Normal people don't start businesses. If entrepreneurs were like everyone else, then there wouldn't be startups and we wouldn't enjoy the game-changing innovations they bring to the world.

And on the 8th day, God created entrepreneurs to keep existing firms from being arrogant and complacent.

References

Chapter One:
[1] Daniel Isenberg, "Entrepreneurs and the Cult of Failure." *Harvard Business Review,* April, 2011, p. 26. Used with permission of the *Harvard Business Review.*
[2] "Nerd of the Amazon" *60 Minutes*, February 3, 1999, CBS video.
[3] Ibid.
[4] Edgar Schein, "How Can Organizations Learn Faster? The Challenge of Entering the Green Room." *Sloan Management Review*, Winter, 1993, p. 87.
[5] "Lucas and Spielberg on Norman Rockwell" *CBS Sunday Morning*, July 4, 2010.
[6] Robert G. Cooper, *Winning at New Products: Creating Value Through Innovation*, (Basic Books, 2011).

Chapter Two:
[7] Michel Lazerow, "Why Weirdos Outperform Normals," March 24, 2013. Michael Lazerow is a LinkedIn Influencer. His article originally appeared in: http://www.linkedin.com/today/post/article/20130324141810-1714080-why-weirdos-outperform-normals
[8] From *DELIVERING HAPPINESS* by Tony Hsieh, p. 165. Copyright © by Tony Hsieh. By permission of Grand Central Publishing. All rights reserved.
[9] Lesley Hazelton, "Jeff Bezos" *Success*, July, 1998, p. 58.
[10] Used by permission of Tom Peters. Go to www.tompeters.com for additional ideas from Tom Peters.
[11] If you are interested in learning more about the need for firms to evolve then my book, *The Ever-Evolving Enterprise.*
[12] Used by permission of Tom Peters. Go to www.tompeters.com for additional ideas from Tom Peters.

Chapter Three:
[13] List found at http://www.brainyquote.com/quotes/keywords/crazy_4.html#42HHR gfQGS3mT8Dg.99
[14] Stephen C. Harper, *The McGraw-Hill Guide to Managing Growth*

in Your Emerging Business, McGraw-Hill, 1994, p. 70.
[15] Meg Cadoux Hirshberg, "I Thought I Knew You." *Inc.* May 2013, p. 41 and 42. Used with permission of *Inc.* magazine.
[16] Deniz Ucgasaran, Paul Westhead, and Mike Wright, "Why Serial Entrepreneurs Don't Learn From Failure." *Harvard Business Review*, April, 2011, p. 26. Used with permission of the *Harvard Business Review.*
[17] Wilson Harrell, *For Entrepreneurs Only*, (Hawthorne, New Jersey, Career Press, 1995) p. 18.
[18] Screenplay for *Legends of the Fall* by Susan Shilliday and Bill Wittliff.
[19] "Nerd of the Amazon," ibid.
[20] *Entrepreneurs*, produced by Nathan Tyler Productions, Waltham Mass, 1986.
[21] "Jet Blue," *60 Minutes*, June 18, 2003, CBS video.
[22] Norm Brodsky "You Do What?" *Inc.* Magazine, February 2008, p. 59. Used with permission of *Inc.* magazine.
[23] Lesley Hazelton, ibid.
[24] "Nerd of the Amazon," ibid.
[25] Margaret Heffernan, "How to Survive Working for a Narcissistic Leader." CBS Money Watch, May 19, 2011. Used with permission by Margaret Heffernan – includes some editing and reformatting.

Steve Jobs was known for wrapping up his new product launch presentations with "One more thing."

So here is my "One 'last' thing."

Are you one of the Crazy Ones?

Notes

Notes

Notes

www.ingramcontent.com/pod-product-compliance
Lightning Source LLC
Chambersburg PA
CBHW051322170526
45166CB00002B/647